SALT OF THE EARTH

Salt of the Earth

AN INFORMAL PROFILE
OF RICHARD CARDINAL CUSHING

By John H. Fenton

COWARD-McCANN, Inc.
New York

FOR MARGERY
a practical saint

Contents

*Illustrations will be found following
pages 52 and 180*

Preface

THIS safari into the field of biography after more than thirty-seven years of daily newspapering in Boston would not have been possible without the help of some good friends, most of them in my own vineyard. It all began with an assignment from Harrison E. Salisbury, assistant managing editor of *The New York Times,* to do a "take out" on the Roman Catholic Archbishop of Boston, who suddenly seemed to have burst on the national scene as a part of the John F. Kennedy legend. The day the piece appeared, February 6, 1964, a telephone call from Coward-McCann, Inc., suggested the possibility of expanding it into an informal, anecdotal biography. It seemed like a reasonable suggestion. Boston newspaper files bulged with clippings and the city apparently teemed with clerics and lay people who had known Richard Cushing from away back. But it didn't work out that way.

The newspaper clippings were voluminous, all right, and they provided a wealth of contemporary reports of the Cardinal's public appearances, and even a semblance of biographical material at the time of his becoming a bishop, in 1939. But they showed an implied censorship that marked the influence of a powerful figure in the community. And seemingly garrulous Boston Irish—priests, bankers, lawyers, politicians—became strangely tongue tied. It was five months after the project got under way before the Cardinal would consent to a personal interview, and then he was as pleasant and as gracious as one could ask. But national magazine articles before and shortly after the interview apparently vexed him no end and his Eminence withdrew into his self-imposed Coventry.

But for all that, I think he genuinely shuns personal publicity; although he would do almost anything to help promote his charitable work, and that if he had his way, he would go to South America and end his days as a missionary, as he has at least twice tried to do unsuccessfully in appeals to Rome. Richard Cushing has said he does not understand himself, and certainly few others do, either, with the possible exception of Pope John, who gave him the red hat of a cardinal.

What follows, then, is an unauthorized biographical profile of a Christian shepherd who can wield his liturgical crozier as a goad or protective staff with equal effectiveness; a lonely, unpredictable soul who perhaps was born fifty years too soon, but unleashed by the ecumenical spirit of Pope John is aware of the potentiality of the Roman Catholic Church's new Pentecost in terms of a united flock, while continuing his personal struggle with being a Boston Irishman set down in the capital of Yankee Puritanism. If the image remains cloudy, then, so, too, is the spirit of ecumenism.

Indebtedness is acknowledged to his Eminence for a fleeting hour in July, 1964. Thanks go also to Monsignor Francis J. Lally, editor of the *Pilot*; his assistant, Father

John J. Grant, and to George E. Ryan, lay director of the archdiocesan news bureau, as well as to just about every Boston newspaperman and woman who has covered the Cardinal in the last twenty-five years. The list specifically should include Edward G. McGrath, George Croft, the late Joseph Dinneen and the late Ray McPartlin, all of the Boston *Globe*; Fred Brady, Joseph T. Sullivan, Peter Barnicle and William J. McCarthy of the Boston *Herald*, and Father "Joe Mack" of the *Traveler*. I am equally grateful to the morgue keepers of the *Globe* and of the *Herald*, and to Walter Muir Whitehill, director of the Boston Athenaeum.

Paul Ganley of the *Traveler* did much of the dogged research in the clippings. Monsignors George W. Casey and Edward G. Murray, the Rev. T. C. Whitehouse of the Massachusetts Council of Churches, Robert E. Segal of the Jewish Community Council, Robert Johnson of the Sudbury Methodist Church, Warren Carberg of the Methodist News Bureau and Abbie Ziffren of the National Desk at the *Times* all played special resource roles. And to put it all together, the final manuscript was lovingly typed between household chores by Priscilla Ann Abercrombie, a filial relative of mine who also is maternal custodian of three of my grandchildren.

JOHN H. FENTON

Andover, Massachusetts
December, 1964

SALT OF THE EARTH

CHAPTER I

Boston's Prince of the Church

ON a chilly Saturday morning in January 1964, television crews, newspapermen, and a handful of spectators gathered in the soot-stained Gothic Cathedral of the Holy Cross in Boston to watch a final rehearsal of Mozart's Requiem Mass in D Minor. Priests of the Roman Catholic Church and masters of choral and symphonic music combined their talents as craftsmen in a grieving city's memorial tribute to a native son and martyred President. It was a scene that would have been appreciated by John F. Kennedy, himself a craftsman in the art of politics, in whose memory the mass was to be performed the following day, before an audience of 1,800 persons in the cathedral and millions of television watchers across the nation.

Erich Leinsdorf, wearing black slacks and a black velveteen Eisenhower jacket, conducted the Boston Symphony Orchestra. The Boston Pro Musica, the Harvard Glee Club, the Radcliffe Choral Society, the New England Conservatory of Music and the choir of St. John's Seminary, 180 voices in all, joined with four soloists in the musical accompaniment to the liturgy of the mass.

Dominating it all was the Most Rev. Richard James Cushing, Cardinal Archbishop of 1,777,284 Catholics in the Boston Archdiocese. With a smile of reassurance for singers awed by the setting and with an occasional unecclesiastical pleasantry for anyone within earshot, the gaunt, white-haired prelate in street clerical garb moved around the altar, simulating with assisting priests the memorial mass, keenly aware of the tensions that were rising.

As one who had served the spiritual needs of John F. Kennedy in triumph and in grief, Cardinal Cushing probably carried a heavier burden of sorrow than any one else at the rehearsal. But it was masked behind the hollow eyes of his deeply lined face as he concerned himself with seeing that no one else cracked.

At last, the words of the mass and the musical score ended. For a moment, priests and musicians alike seemed to freeze like so many wax figures, their drawn faces reflecting fatigue. But the tall prelate already was moving toward a lectern in front of the high altar, where he leaned his elbows, as if to offer a few words of praise and encouragement.

Instead, the dry, nasal voice solemnly intoned:

"We shall now take up the collection."

There was a sharp pause, as if everyone in the cathedral had drawn in his breath as one. High in the vaulted ceiling, the tasseled red hat once worn by William Cardinal O'Connell stirred in an eddy of cold air. It had been hung there on his death in 1944, to remain until it disintegrated, as a symbol of the mortality of man.

Then, from the floor below there welled up a fountain of laughter. The eyes of Cardinal Cushing twinkled as he saw the tension dissolve. It was the sort of impulsive gesture

4

that has motivated the prelate during the twenty years of his administration of the archdiocese.

The newspapermen present long since had ceased to be surprised by the unpredictable cardinal. In fact, Robert Hassett of the Boston *Herald* wrote for the next morning's paper, "Jack Kennedy would have laughed with the rest, at a good joke to end a good day's work."

But the Cardinal's gesture must have come as a surprise to many of the others, especially the Friends of the Boston Symphony, who generally represented Proper Protestant Boston, though two of them, Henry B. Cabot, president of the Symphony, and Erich Leinsdorf, music director, might have anticipated it.

Mr. Cabot, bearer of a venerable Boston Yankee name, had conceived the idea of having the Symphony play at some sort of memorial service. Not knowing the Cardinal, he approached him through an intermediary, Monsignor Edward G. Murray.

A quarter of a century earlier, the austere Cardinal O'Connell would hardly have sanctioned the fusing of secular music with the ritual of the mass within his own cathedral, much less consider such a proposal from anyone else. But Cardinal Cushing was enthusiastic from the outset. When he was introduced to Mr. Cabot he thrust out his hand and exclaimed, "Hello, Henry!" Mr. Cabot was delighted.

Just before the rehearsal got under way, Cardinal Cushing approached Mr. Leinsdorf.

"Good luck to you," he said. "I'll do the best I can, but I don't know much about music and I've got a voice like a fish peddler."

Mr. Leinsdorf replied, "Your Eminence, it's the heart that counts, rather than the voice."

Cushing's voice, strained by more than forty years of preaching in churches and halls of inferior acoustical qualities, and further rasped by chronic asthma, is penetrating and nasal, and his diction is peppered with the "disses" and "dats" that bespeak his South Boston Irish origin. It has become increasingly familiar since he became an archbishop in 1944 both to the Catholics of his large diocese and since 1958 to Boston Protestants and Jews, in whose churches and synagogues, once off limits to any Catholic clergyman, he has been a frequent guest speaker. His efforts to bridge the gulf between Boston's Catholics and the rest of the community long antedate the Second Vatican Council. Professor George H. Williams, of the Harvard Divinity School, who served as a Protestant observer at the first session of the Council called by Pope John, commented that although many prelates had been converted by the spirit of the Pontiff, "Cardinal Cushing long anticipated and implemented in his diocese the pastoral and ecumenical principles of Pope John's pontificate and council."

With the rise of John F. Kennedy, whose spiritual adviser he was, the Cardinal was thrust onto the stage of contemporary political history; and when the memorial mass to the late President was performed from the cathedral on January 19, 1964, the cracked Cushing voice became known to millions. Cardinal Cushing himself, despite the firm stand he has taken on a number of vital church issues, despite his willingness to speak at great length in public, his friendliness toward newspapermen and his assiduous use of all the means of publicity at his command—radio, TV, and the diocese's weekly newspaper—remains an enigmatic, contradictory, and unpredictable figure even in his own archdiocese.

He makes frequent trips but when he is in Boston, he is

on the radio three times daily for a recitation of the Rosary from the archepiscopal residence. Between times, he makes visits to parishes for confirmations or dedications or cornerstone ceremonies. A telephone call to news desks in Boston newspapers or television and radio offices about some special function will bring photographers and reporters to cover the event. Protestants used to be irked by this, but now they appreciate the value of mass communications. As for the Cardinal, he has said that if St. Paul were preaching today he would not hesitate to make use of every available means of spreading his message.

A tall, gaunt man of sixty-nine whose youthful solidity has been consumed by illnesses and an incredible zeal for work, he thinks nothing of putting in an 18-hour day, not merely in his study or at the altar, but in innumerable public appearances which require him to rush by car from one end of his archdiocese to the other, to fly to Rome or go halfway across the country to celebrate a church observance. His travels are never periods of rest; the closest he ever comes to relaxation is to take an annual trip to Camp Drum, N.Y., when the Massachusetts National Guard is on summer maneuvers and he goes to check up on his chaplains. Then, clad in unmarked field fatigues, he disappears to a remote area of a mock battleground where there are no reporters.

In recent years he has amused audiences with personal anecdotes about his early life; but he has maintained in general a strict silence on personal matters and also exercised censorship over members of his family as well. While he has allowed individual reporters to interview him, he has observed long periods of reticence as a result. He seemed to be flattered if somewhat nonplused when a group of Daughters of St. Paul, a society of book-publish-

7

ing nuns, surprised him with a biography on his sixty-ninth birthday in 1964, explaining that they had used a hidden tape recorder for six years whenever they could get near him. But the Cardinal became furious over a cover story in *Time* magazine a few months later, and accused the editors of slanting the article "in accordance with a preconceived plan" that gave a false impression of him. The *Pilot*, the diocese's weekly paper, followed with an editorial along the same lines. Subsequently the Cardinal managed to abort another magazine article on his seminary for delayed vocations to the priesthood by warning the rector that "they'll make a fool of you."

Yet as a public speaker he unbends to the point of garrulity, and becomes so rambling that one former baseball reporter assigned to the religion beat has compared him to Casey Stengel, the loquacious manager of the New York Mets. The Cardinal is aware of his reputation as a talker; he once wrote in the *Pilot*, "As most of you know, I am a man of a few million words.

"Someone told me," he went on, "that I am fine for about fifteen minutes, but when I get to the half hour mark you are more interested in physical survival than spiritual sustenance." He said he would bring along a timekeeper to strike a gong after fifteen minutes; but has never gotten around to that reform. On one occasion, a drum and bugle corps competition, Cushing's speech went on for so long that, accidentally or otherwise, it was finally drowned out when one band struck up a rousing march.

Heavy though his public speaking schedule was, it was almost doubled shortly after his return from the second session of the Vatican Council. He told a gathering at St. Benedict's Parish in Somerville that he would be speaking in Protestant churches. "Nothing like this has ever happened

8

before," he said. "I am accepting invitations from ministers and will make these talks in the ecumenical spirit." Soon after the Cardinal was addressing groups in Protestant churches and parish halls, as well as Jewish congregations; and the long rambling talks, larded with the personal touches and apparently irrelevant asides so familiar to his Catholic listeners, beguiled his new audiences with spiritual pleas for brotherly love and doubled them up with earthy laughter.

It is, in fact, Richard Cushing more than any other single person who has helped to thaw the religious climate of Boston, once the capital of Protestant Puritanism with a subculture of Irish Catholic immigrants who were kept firmly in their own low social status. Cushing's predecessor, William Cardinal O'Connell, was credited with bringing the church out of the catacombs in Boston; but he was a cold, scholarly, austere prelate who accepted Protestants by sufferance. A man of ample girth, he affected wide flowing robes that occasionally billowed out to force passersby to give way or step into the gutter as he strolled along downtown Tremont Street receiving the obeisance of the faithful. Irreverently, if sometimes affectionately, called "Gangplank Bill," Cardinal O'Connell frequently was photographed moving up or down a steamship gangplank, bound on his travels. Every year as the New England blizzards began to descend, the old cardinal would embark for Nassau in the Bahamas to his winter residence—because, it was sometimes remarked behind the hand, he could not bear to see his poor parishioners shiver in the cold—the sort of comment engendered by the religious climate of Boston.

Cardinal Cushing, on the other hand, keeps returning to Boston as soon as possible from his trips, being much in demand as a speaker. He deprecates his ecclesiastical robes as "haberdashery," and dispenses with the kissing of the episcopal ring whenever he can, outside of churches. He embraces believers as well as unbelievers and is held in higher esteem in some Protestant circles than among the latter-day snobs of his own religious persuasion.

But for all his hearty, informal manners, his apparent accessibility, and his genuinely ecumenical spirit, the Cardinal can be a crusty old curmudgeon. It may be due partly to his native Irish temper, or to an irritability brought on by his many serious illnesses ranging from chronic asthma and emphysema to ulcers and prostatic cancer; but in any case Cardinal Cushing has a faculty for keeping people at arm's length, as if he wants it understood that no one "owns" him. A county sheriff with an impressive talent for raising money may earn a hearty slap on the back one week and find himself cut dead the next. Even Joseph P. Kennedy has not been immune to the archepiscopal disapprobation. Once when he made a sizable donation toward a hospital for chronically ill children in memory of his own son, Joseph P. Kennedy Jr., the Cardinal did not hesitate to let it be known that the amount fell far short of furnishing the institution. In fact, it is said that the Cardinal is capable of using language that would arouse the admiration of a longshoreman when someone makes a donation less than what he thinks the donor is good for.

Yet when Robert F. Kennedy, then Attorney General, needed a million dollars or so for ransom after the Cuban fiasco, he appealed to Cardinal Cushing—who, in turn, has sources to which he can appeal, although he takes patent delight in referring to the dimes, quarters and half dollars that come in from the Irish of South Boston from which the Cardinal came.

In addition to his charity fund, which serves as a broad

umbrella for his many activities, Cardinal Cushing also administers a multimillion-dollar archdiocese whose property is all listed under the name of "The Roman Catholic Archbishop of Boston" as a corporation sole. The property includes the facilities of one of the most extensive and best-equipped Catholic parochial school systems in the county, hospitals, rehabilitation centers and seminaries, as well as convents and church buildings.

Yet to characterize the Cardinal merely as the custodian of immense power and property would be to emphasize only one facet of a man of international interests. Although by virtue of his position as spiritual leader of nearly a third of all the people in eastern Massachusetts, Cardinal Cushing holds tremendous power, he is known to realize that his power is great only so long as he does not wield it. Instead, he accomplishes most of his aims by the inference of his power, although his name has sometimes been used without official sanction. He has never publicly endorsed a political candidate except in 1960 when he pleaded the cause of John F. Kennedy in his race for President in the interests of overcoming the religious issue raised by Kennedy's opponents. Legislative leaders might call on the Cardinal for advice, and he might give it, at the same time counseling them to use their own best judgment. When he does become interested in a moral issue, such as the birth control referendum which he opposed in 1958, his views are expressed editorially in the *Pilot*, the archdiocan weekly.

His positions on political matters have baffled Protestants and loyal Catholics, and even experts who are accustomed to the self-contradictions of lay politicians. In the Church he is an outstanding progressive, but he stands staunchly with the right wing in his opposition to Communism. He has endorsed the John Birch Society, though he has partly retreated from this position after learning of the society's extremist views and tactics. Yet he is a life member of the N.A.A.C.P., a foe of racial prejudice, and an advocate of civil rights; and the apparent conflict between these positions has never been logically explained.

The Cardinal readily confesses that he was a high school dropout and that his Latin scholarship is so faulty that Protestant observers at the Vatican Council, with their interpreters, knew more of what was going on than he did. Yet he emerged as a progressive leader of extraordinary stature at that conclave of scholars. In spite of his youthful difficulties with book work, he was twice on the point of entering the Society of Jesus, which requires more than average scholastic ability of its postulants; he has never given a firm reason for his turning from a Jesuit vocation, but he has always shown a deep admiration for the order.

As for the scholars and theologians, Cardinal Cushing holds that the ecumenical spirit of unity will never work "until they bring it down to the little people, like you and me, who may not know much about faith, but they love God and they are the salt of the earth."

It was perhaps his feeling for the "little people" from whom he sprang that commended him to Pope John XXIII, who made Cushing a cardinal in 1958. Ordained a priest in 1921, Cushing was made auxiliary bishop to the ailing Cardinal O'Connell in 1939 and named temporary administrator of the diocese five years later at the death of his superior. By the end of that year he had been elevated to the rank of archbishop, largely, it is said, through the efforts of another native Bay Stater, Francis Cardinal Spellman of New York. Later, a coolness attributed to temperamental differences developed between the two and it was said that Spellman successfully blocked further advancement for Cushing until Pope John XXIII came along. Spellman and Cushing have become friendly again, even though some believe that Cardinal Spellman has reservations about the amount of international publicity that his Boston colleague has received. In any case, possibly because of Pope John's similar humble origins, he recognized Cushing's worth.

"Of the two or three Popes I have known," Cardinal Cushing has said, "Good Pope John was the only one who understood me, and I don't understand myself."

It is Pope John's general views on Christian unity and freedom of religion that Cardinal Cushing has espoused at the Vatican Council; and increasingly since his elevation to the Sacred College of Cardinals he has applied these principles in his own diocese.

His own diocese and his own people have been closest to his heart; yet repeatedly throughout his career and even during the reign of Pope John, Cardinal Cushing has asked to be relieved of his titles and responsibilities to work as a missionary in foreign lands—specifically South America. Possibly in the grinding poverty and illiteracy of underprivileged people Cardinal Cushing sees the qualities that made the Church so important to the Irish immigrants of South Boston in their struggle to rise above their lot and stand as equals with the Yankees on Beacon Hill.

CHAPTER II

Youth in South Boston

WHEN Richard James Cushing was born August 23, 1895, South Boston was as Irish as Cobh, from which many of its inhabitants had sailed as steerage passengers bound for the New World. The second- and third-generation descendants of the peasants who had fled the potato famine overflowed the tenements which had been hastily erected by profiteering Yankee landlords; the saloons overflowed with disillusioned teamsters and dockhands, and the hearts of their priests overflowed with anguish that there were not more hours in the day to care for their flocks.

Richard was the first son and third child of Patrick and Mary Cushing. Patrick had come over from Glenworth in County Cork, and found work as a blacksmith in the trolley car repair pits not far from the cold-water flat at 808 East Third Street where he and Mary made their home for some years. Mary was a Dahill from County Waterford, who was working in Boston as a hired girl for $2 a week when she married Patrick. They were typical of the immigrants who lived in South Boston at the turn of the century.

The district was a pleasant peninsula which jutted out into the Atlantic Ocean and formed one of the sheltering arms of Boston Harbor. It was once intended to be a bedroom suburb for well-to-do Bostonians seeking an escape from the city proper, and some of its streets, down toward City Point, had been laid out to provide wide roadways for carriage traffic and narrow ones for mews. But South Boston never caught on as a fashionable address; the Boston Brahmins preferred Beacon Hill until its summit was razed to help fill in the Back Bay area. Instead, since South Boston was close to the central waterfront, wharves began to spread around the northern rim of the peninsula; and behind them, machine shops and factories that fed on raw materials delivered from the wharves. So it became an industrial district, and the home of the Irish immigrants who could find jobs there during the boom of the Civil War and live in two-decker row houses and three-decker tenements. The Boston Fire of 1872 and the razing of Fort Hill drove others, some of them Irish, into the south peninsula; and joined by succeeding waves of immigrants from Ireland they formed a populous and homogeneous community of workingmen who earned from $9 to $12 a week to support their large families.

As early as 1866 South Boston had become so densely populated that it was divided into two Roman Catholic parishes. The older one, Saints Peter and Paul, served the western half of the district, while the newly created one, Gate of Heaven, served the eastern half. Richard James Cushing was baptized in the rectory of Gate of Heaven Church by Father Thomas J. Brannan on a hot August day following his birth.

Patrick Cushing was making $18 a week in the trolley car shops, working ten hours a day seven days a week, better paid actually than motormen or conductors, for all their fancy buttons. He was remembered as a quiet man, who might stop off for a beer on the way home but apparently did not hang around the saloon long. He was once described as having "the gift of reticence, rare in an Irishman."

Mary Cushing might stop at the grocer's returning from daily mass. If she happened to lack a penny or two of what the groceries cost, she would trudge home and back to pay up the correct amount so that she would not be running up bills. Eventually her family grew to five, and Mary Cushing needed all her talent for stretching dollars to keep them well fed. Cardinal Cushing has remarked that his own talent for handling money may have been inherited from his mother. As archbishop in later years, he always insisted that new churches, schools and other diocesan buildings be free of debt before they were dedicated.

The Irish who were driven from the Ould Sod by famine may have been peasants but they were not sharecroppers. If they brought with them only elementary skills and the legendary pick and shovel, they were independent and lived decently on the low wages they could get in the prosperous Yankee city. They were tough by training and inheritance and the struggle for existence in the slums of the New World. The men were teamsters or "dock wallopers" or dig-and-toss laborers; the girls, waiting for the day when their men could afford to get married, worked as cooks and maids in town, as Mary Dahill had done. Although they slept in garrets, or got up in the cold dawn if they "lived out," they attended mass regularly, and most of their employers' wives kept them under stern supervision and required them to get in at a decent hour when their young men came to take them walking. As Irish families came up in the world to become contractors who hired newer immigrants to do the menial labor, they advanced to "F.I.F.'s" (Fine Irish Families) ; once "shanty Irish," they became "lace-curtain" or, in a later day, two-bathroom or venetian-blind Irish. They made their way up through education; as a new generation had an opportunity for more schooling, they took examinations to become policemen, firemen or letter carriers instead of laborers. Later further advancement became possible through politics and the Church. In its heyday as an Irish stronghold, South Boston is said to have produced more priests and nuns than any comparable section of the United States; and it was a mark of respectability for one or more of the numerous sons and daughters of Irish families to choose the religious life.

The lives of the laity were never far from the Church, and when young Richard Cushing, a gangling, freckle-faced boy with dark unruly hair, had done his home chores —chopping wood, carrying coal, running errands, cleaning carpets—he would go down to the church to see if he could help the Father with the lawn, shovel snow, or give the church a good going over before Sunday mass. He was a particularly faithful assistant to the janitor of St. Eulalia's church while Father Mortimer E. Toomey was pastor. As for the recreation of South Boston Irish boys, this consisted of what they could find for themselves—swimming, skating or ball playing. In later years, dedicating a new recreational center for teen-agers, Cardinal Cushing remarked that when he was young no one made a project of recreations; the boys formed their own plans and executed them.

Immobilized between the waterfront and Back Bay, the impregnable citadel of Puritan Anglo-Saxon Boston, the

Irish created a society of their own within the community. Protestant Boston was culturally English; the Catholic Irish were Anglophobes. Proper Boston was well established; its first families had amassed their fortunes some time before the Irish had begun to arrive as immigrants, and had already founded many of their lasting institutions, including their schools and colleges. As Samuel Eliot Morison has pointed out, the Bostonians did not make money for its own sake (like such outlanders as the Rockefellers or the Mellons). They made it to establish a society that was circumscribed by such institutions as Groton, Harvard, Trinity Church and the Somerset Club. While proper Boston recognized the devotion of the Catholic Irish to their faith, the respectability of most of their poor families, and was only too glad to have their sons as laborers and their daughters as household help, it never let down the social barriers.

The suspicion between the two social groups was mutual, and on both sides it was, in large measure, due to the bigotry of the less educated elements. Yet fusty old Cardinal O'Connell was a close friend of Episcopal Bishop William Appleton Lawrence. But bigotry flourished throughout the nineteenth century; at one time, before the Civil War, Negroes did not want Irishmen, who might be a threat to their jobs, living on the same street with them.

Though South Boston and Back Bay remained worlds apart until the mid-twentieth century, the Irish could and did rise economically and politically.

From the time that Hugh O'Brien became the first Catholic mayor of Boston, in 1844, and on through the day that John Boyle O'Reilly landed there after fleeing from an English penal colony in 1889, the Irish developed a fine sense for American politics, whetted in the old country, and honed to a cutting edge by observing the flinty Yankees. In fact, Malcolm Nichols was the last Protestant to be elected mayor thirty years ago.

Politics was an outlet that opened up and spread city-wide as votes gave the Irish a voice that the social position of the Protestants could not silence. And it led eventually to jobs for constituents and a new kind of respectability for the city alderman and state representative and his family.

Among the tribal customs that were brought over and nurtured in the New World was the wake. This was the practice, when death visited a family, to have at least one of the surviving members sit up through at least two nights with the body of the loved one, as it was laid out in the parlor. The neighbors brought in food, tears and condolence.

During the nights, the men might gravitate to the kitchen for talk and perhaps a touch of whiskey. And sandwiches and coffee or tea were to be had for grieving friends and visiting politicians. Any politician with the least sense of duty would no more think of missing any wake in his district than he would Sunday mass.

Sometime during each evening, the priest would come by and lead those in the parlor in the Rosary. No matter what sort of a life the departed might have led, he was a saint until after the funeral mass on the third morning. One of the stories that is still told in South Boston is of the gang foreman who could only say to the widow of one of his ditch diggers, "Pat was a good shoveler; not a fancy shoveler, mind you, but a good shoveler."

And more than one election was swung as the result of votes solicited in hallway or kitchen while the women were keening in the parlor and the guttering candles cast flickering shadows on the waxen features of the corpse.

The rise of the Irish in politics inevitably involved them in corruption; and the deterioration of parts of the industrial districts brought on slum conditions that spawned gangs of hoodlums. Yet for every hoodlum there were a hundred like Mary Dahill Cushing who went to mass every day and a hundred sober decent workingmen like Patrick Cushing; and for every cigar-chewing, derby-hatted ward heeler of the rougher days there were another hundred like John W. McCormack. Not all of them could become Speaker of the House of Representatives, as he did, but they were his constituents; they were respectable men who, if they did not become priests, marched in Holy Name parades to communion breakfasts.

Even though the Irish have risen in the world to become wealthy and prominent in civic and political affairs and to alter the social structure of the Establishment in Boston, the clannishness by which they organized their subcommunity within a Protestant culture has remained. The Irish insisted on their independent agencies, organized on Catholic principles, in order to preserve their subculture and take care of their own.

It was in such an atmosphere of clannishness and Celtic solidarity that Richard Cushing grew up. In a similar community, East Boston, another Irish immigrant family, named Kennedy, settled long enough to parlay the profits from a saloon into the foundation of a fortune that led them to fame and position elsewhere.

In Richard Cushing's boyhood, the Irish community was not a wealthy one and parochial schools were few. Richard went to public school, and on a June day in 1908, clad in a white starched shirt and knickerbockers, was one of a class of 125 which was graduated from Oliver Hazard Perry Grammar School. The girls, in ruffled dresses, hair ribbons and high-buttoned shoes, giggled during the shuffling for position before the class picture was to be taken. Finally, one teacher, running her eyes along the line, spoke up:

"Richard Cushing, step to the right, Alice Ware's hair ribbons are blocking your face. If you're not in the picture, how are your classmates going to remember you?"

One old tad on the police force, seeing Cushing return one day years later in the robes of a bishop, remembered him and whispered hoarsely, "You've come a long way, Dickie boy, since I used to boot you one on Broadway!"

Richard Cushing went on in the fall to South Boston High School. But after piling up an impressive record for truancy, he dropped out of school before the end of the year. As he cleaned out his locker, he grumbled, "I've had enough of this place."

The archives of South Boston High School do not preserve the record of Cushing's truancy. The day he was named archbishop, a teacher at the school recalled that the new prelate had been a chronic stay-out. The principal, finding the record in the file, tore it up and dropped the pieces into his wastebasket.

Years later, Richard Cushing credited Monsignor Richard B. Cushion, a cousin of his father's, with getting him back on the educational track. But it is certainly true that any notion young Cushing might have had of quitting school for good did not take into account the iron will of Father Toomey. The priest was one of a stalwart breed of parish padres that has faded into history along with spike-chewing top sergeants, dyspeptic city editors and birch rod schoolmasters. He was fully cognizant of the educational shortcomings and childlike faith of most of the Irish immigrants in his flock. In things spiritual and moral, and sometimes political, his word was law. For example, he looked on roller coasters and merry-go-rounds as vehicles of the devil incarnate and kept them forever out of South Boston to preserve its integrity.

Father Toomey apparently saw something in his faithful assistant janitor and decided to keep an eye on him. Keeping an eye on any fourteen-year-old boy takes doing, but with the help of his curate, Father Jeremiah E. Driscoll, and supported by his intuition and his obstinacy, Father Toomey had his way. When fall arrived, young Cushing was enrolled at Boston College High School.

Tuition at the parochial school was $60 a year, which meant that young Dick Cushing would have to find some part-time work. During the summer, he got a job as a timekeeper on some construction work on the waterfront. His father, with a rare few moments of time off, came over one afternoon to see how his son was getting along. At about the time he arrived, a bell diver emerged from the water. Pat Cushing grinned.

"If I had known you could do that, I would have walked all the way over myself," he commented.

In the fall, shortly after school opened, Dick Cushing was tapped to serve mass for one of the priests. With his faulty Latin, he managed to bungle the responses, and this led to other errors. Afterward, in the sacristy, the distraught priest turned to Cushing and said, acidly, "I won't ask you if you have ever served mass before, young man, I'll just ask if you have ever been to mass before!"

But if he was deficient in Latin at that period, Dick

Cushing enjoyed debating. This led to his taking the stump for older pals who were entering politics. He even spoke at one time for James Michael Curley, who came from Roxbury, and went on to become one of the most colorful of the old-time political bosses.

One political speech, when he was sixteen years old, probably was the turning point of the Cushing career. He was standing on the tailboard of a wagon, a favorite podium of old-time campaigners, exhorting a crowd to vote for Dan Casey, who was running for state representative.

Down the street came Father Toomey. He took one look at the figure on the tailboard and began flailing his way through the crowd. His eyes blazing with indignation, the priest reached up and grabbed Dick Cushing by the ankles, pulled him to the street and kicked him firmly in the rear.

"You'll either be a priest or a politician," roared Father Toomey. "Make up your mind!"

This was as close as Richard Cushing ever came to an orthodox political career. From that moment, he set his course for the priesthood. But for all his good intentions, he found himself in scholastic straits in the winter of his junior year at the Jesuit high school. A letter to his father from the prefect of studies interrupted the routine of the Cushing household one bitter night in January, 1912.

"Never mind the stew, Mary," said Pat Cushing after reading the letter. "We'd best get started, Richard, and put on your rubbers, it's starting to snow."

The father and son sat shivering and silent in a streetcar that took them to the rectory in town. They were shown into a shabby reception room, where a young priest greeted them. The two men talked, and Richard Cushing listened.

"After all, Mr. Cushing," the priest said finally, "God

calls his children to many vocations, few to the life of the intellect and fewer still to the dignity of His priesthood."

"It could be, Father, he's been working too hard weekends for Father Toomey," Patrick Cushing offered in his son's defense.

"No question of that," said the young priest, rising to end the interview, "and you shouldn't feel too bad about it at all. St. Joseph was a carpenter and God will find work for this son of yours."

As they made the cold ride back, young Cushing burst out with the impetuousness of sixteen years, "They can have their diploma. I'll get a job and help at home."

With the final clang of the motorman's bell at City Point, Patrick Cushing turned to his son and said, "Do the best you can, 'tis all God asks; he'll do the rest. Carry on."

Doggedly, and with help from Fathers Toomey and Driscoll, Dick Cushing made the grade. When the Boston College High School Class of 1913 was graduated, he not only received his diploma, but he also was picked to make one of the speeches. It was on "The Press as an Intellectual Force."

That fall, Dick Cushing entered Boston College as a freshman. One morning, on the streetcar over from South Boston, he met a first cousin, John P. Kenneally, a night school law student and a daytime adjuster for a state-sponsored workmen's compensation insurance association.

"Dick," he said, "if you swap over to law school, I can get you a swell job with a good future in my outfit. They need more adjusters."

Young Cushing shook his head.

"Not for me," he replied. "I'm going to be a priest."

"A priest!" Kenneally exclaimed. "What do you want to

do that for? What do you get? Three square meals a day, a place to sleep and a lot of hard work, no dough, and you can't even get married."

"I know all that," his cousin agreed, "but it's what I want to do; that's what I've wanted ever since I was a kid."

After two years at Boston College, where his scholastic pace began to pick up, young Cushing transferred to St. John's Seminary to begin the six years it would take to qualify him as a secular priest in the Boston Archdiocese.

On September 26, 1915, Richard Cushing began a regimen that has been his schedule pretty much of the time ever since. It started at 6 A.M., and continued to 9:30 P.M. and although he missed the honors list the first time around, he never failed to make it after that.

Classmates cautiously described him as alert in class and having a droll humor that helped to relieve tensions. One future priest, failing miserably one day in Father John S. Keating's Greek class, slumped miserably into his seat. There was a gravelly whisper from Cushing, across the aisle. "Ah, forget it; tomorrow's another day."

Years afterward, as he was receiving an honorary degree from Boston College, Richard Cushing, by then a bishop, spotted Father Keating on the platform. In the same low growl, he said, "You know, of all people, Father, that I don't deserve this."

In his first year at seminary, Dick Cushing was assigned to duties with the student branch of the Society for the Propagation of the Faith. It was a prophetic moment. The society was founded in 1819 by a young French girl, Pauline Marie Jaricot of Lyons, as a means of raising funds for missions, especially in America. Members were expected to say one Our Father and one Hail Mary every day for the society and to put aside at least a penny a week. Although started as an endeavor of the laity, Cardinal O'Connell of Boston eventually had it taken over by the clergy in the interests of closer supervision and fiscal control. The Cardinal was one of the old school in the Roman Church, who held that authority should come from the top down in ecclesiastical matters. The world headquarters are now centered in Rome, but district offices have autonomy to serve as they see fit. Every branch of the organization in the field was expected to contribute part of its revenue to the home office, although there were no set quotas. The United States was considered a missionary land until well after the turn of the century and was a principal beneficiary of the society until 1918; in a period of fifteen years while Benedict J. Fenwick was bishop of Boston, the diocese received a total of $46,639.

But when Richard Cushing joined the organization as a seminarian, the tide began to turn. He had a natural and brilliant talent for fund raising, which has been conspicuous throughout his career in the Church, and soon he was coaxing dimes and nickels out of the thin pockets of his fellow students for the benefit of missions abroad. It was the start of his reputation in the Church as the "Bishop of the Missions."

Normally some of Cushing's class at the seminary would have been selected for special studies at the North American College in Rome. But travel conditions during World War I were too hazardous for ocean voyages, and Cushing's class remained in Boston to finish its studies.

On May 26, 1921, Richard J. Cushing was among twenty-seven young deacons ordained to the priesthood in Holy Cross Cathedral by Cardinal O'Connell. That night, in South Boston, Dan Casey and six other boyhood friends of Cushing gathered for a reunion with the new priest. Each had chipped in a $5 gold piece. In presenting the gift, Dan, now Judge Casey, said, "Dick, here is a token of our esteem, and the next time we meet together it will be to celebrate your getting the red hat."

The following Sunday, Father Cushing celebrated his first mass in his home parish of St. Eulalia's. Both of his parents, three sisters, his brother, his maternal grandmother, an aunt who had held him at his baptism and a host of other relatives were on hand. They moved forward at the close to receive the young priest's first blessings.

The next morning, Father Cushing reported to St. Patrick's Church in Roxbury, within walking distance of his parents' home. But he was there less than two months. He later said that either the pastor did not like him, or he had no flair for parish work. In any event, he was next assigned to St. Benedict's, Somerville. He lasted nine months there, only to find he did not measure up.

A day or two after his dismissal from St. Benedict's, Father Cushing appeared at the door of Cardinal O'Connell's residence, hat in hand, and rang the bell. To his amazement, the majestic figure of the Cardinal appeared as the door opened. The young priest asked permission to speak to his Eminence.

"Have you an appointment?" the portly prelate asked with a disapproving frown.

"No, your Eminence."

"Then how dare you come here without one!"

"Your Eminence, I couldn't be in any worse trouble than I am now, so I thought I'd take heaven by storm!"

If the heavy eyelids flickered, the curate did not notice it.
"Come in," said the Cardinal, shortly.

Leading the way into his study, O'Connell waved Father
Cushing to a chair and sat back to listen. The young priest
poured out his troubles.

"I've been in three parishes in about two and a half
months and I've come to the conclusion I don't belong
here," said the young priest. "I'll never be happy in any of
those parishes; the work is not for me."

"You're not going to be in a parish," said the Cardinal.
"You're supposed to go to the university."

"Oh, I'm not interested in going to the university," Father Cushing replied quickly.

The eyes of the old prelate blinked. Here was a young
priest, fresh out of seminary, selected to do further studying at the Catholic University of America, and already kick-
ing over the traces.

"What do you want?" Cardinal O'Connell asked in slow,
measured tones that bore the rising inflections of an Irish
brogue.

"Well, your Eminence," responded young Cushing,
plunging head-on into the situation of the moment, "I
think I'd like to go to the foreign missions—China or Africa, or join the Marist fathers in the Solomons—
anywhere; I'm big and strong."

"Listen, Tunney," growled the Cardinal, using a current
nickname, "your foreign missions will be where I send
you."

Then, as if by inspiration, the Cardinal reached toward a
pile of correspondence and pulled out a letter. Reading it
briefly, to refresh his memory, the Cardinal peered at the
priest before him.

"Father McGlinchey needs some help over at the office of the Propagation of the Faith; tell him I sent you and to put you to work," he said.

Gratefully, Father Cushing kissed the episcopal ring and left.

CHAPTER III

Priest of the Missions

WHETHER it was chance or foresight which led Cardinal O'Connell to assign a faltering young priest to a relatively obscure function in the Church will never be known. But his directive placed Richard Cushing at the threshold of a career that would shape his destiny. Although he was not to leave his native soil for many years, he was to know and become well known to bishops and missionaries from all over the world who visited Boston within the next two decades. Thousands of priests were to become aware of the benefactions of the Boston office of the Society for the Propagation of the Faith.

Its headquarters were in a single room on the second floor of a brownstone building in the South End. The society's chief function was to raise funds for missions; it did not recruit missionaries or administer specific missions. The director was Father McGlinchey, who had succeeded the Rev. James A. Walsh as director of the Boston branch when Father Walsh resigned to establish what has become the Maryknoll Mission in New York State.

Father McGlinchey and the young priest Cushing hit it

off well from the start. The work of the society was already familiar to Cushing; as a seminarian he had shown a knack for raising funds for it. He found quarters in the rectory of Holy Cross Cathedral, and was able to walk to work. Within weeks, urchins from the area were trooping after the tall young Father Cushing. He was said to be able to spot a worn-out pair of shoes a block away and soon was spending his own meager income keeping youngsters shod. But most of all, they knew that sooner or later he would turn in at a corner candy store, where pennies could buy such bargains as licorice and jawbreakers.

Once, while trudging through a snowstorm on fashionable Arlington Street, Father Cushing saw two nuns who were having an even rougher time combating the storm in their cumbersome habits. He found out that they were on their way to mass at the Church of Notre Dame des Victoires, a good half mile from their convent in the Back Bay. The priest said that if the sisters were agreeable, he would arrange to say mass for them daily at the convent. And for the next eight years, Father Cushing climbed to a small chapel which he had furnished himself, at the top of the house, to say mass.

Later that same winter, as he sat in his office talking with an Oblate father on brief leave from missionary duties in Alaska among the Eskimos, the visitor commented on the cheerful pounding of the radiator as it overcame the chilly blasts outside, and said ruefully that coal in his territory ran as high as $125 a ton.

"That got me out of my chair in a hurry," Father Cushing later told an audience during an exhortation to dig down for the Oblate missionaries in Alaska.

Later, when the society office was moved to Franklin Street, in the business center of the city, Fathers McGlinchey and Cushing had to commute by Elevated. And more than once, Father Cushing had to ask the keeper of the turnstile to trust him until the next day because he had given his last nickel to a panhandler.

For more than twenty years, Father Cushing labored for the society. He and Father McGlinchey would preach at as many as six masses on a Sunday morning in separate parts of the archdiocese. And often they would be on hand to say a few words for missions at a benediction in the afternoon. Their faces became known everywhere there was a Catholic church. And the Cushing voice was particularly remembered and often mimicked by parish wags, although not when he was around.

In 1928, Father Cushing was named director of the society to succeed Father McGlinchey, by then a monsignor, who returned to parish work.

The same year, Father Cushing formed the Sen Fu Club for women, an organization devoted to studying the missile so that the members could carry their knowledge into their own homes and into organizations to which they belonged. Sen Fu is the Chinese equivalent of "father."

A few years later, the society director formed the Father Jim Hennessey Club for men, along the same lines as the Sen Fu. Father Hennessey had lived at the cathedral rectory. Impressed by the work of his colleague, he said one day to Father Cushing, "The foreign missions fields are suffering from lack of priests. It seems to me that the problem could be solved if a number of priests on the home front volunteered to give a limited number of years in the field. I am ready to be the first."

Father Hennessey offered to give five years of his life in the field. He was sent to the North Solomon Islands, in the

Pacific. He never returned. Like many other missionaries, he was engulfed by the Japanese tide in World War II.

But as the war went on, some of the mission harvest began to be gathered by American fighting men. Word came back of natives, riding through jungles on sputtering motorcycles, or commuting among the islands in motorboats, the gifts of American missionaries. And scorning the possibility of reprisals from the Japanese, the natives faithfully served the Americans as scouts and in other useful ways, because, they would explain, "You come from the place of Father Cushing in America."

Field altars and mass kits for chaplains, and other materials poured to the Pacific from Boston as the war rolled on. Before the end of the war, Cushing was known throughout the Church as a leading spirit in the Society for the Propagation of the Faith. But the direction of the Boston branch had shifted to other hands. New duties were pressing in on Richard Cushing. His success as a fund raiser for missions and for the Holy Office and his talents as an administrator did not go unnoticed.

Among the clergy living in the cathedral rectory during Richard Cushing's early years with the society was Monsignor Spellman, a native of Whitman, Massachusetts. He was six years older than Father Cushing and already was assistant chancellor of the archdiocese. Because of his scholastic ability, he had been sent to Rome for special studies at the North American College, and he was ordained to the priesthood in the Eternal City in 1916.

After nine years of varied duties back in Boston, Monsignor Spellman was recalled to Rome to become the first American priest to be attached to the office of the Papal Sec-

33

retary of State, Eugenio Cardinal Pacelli. The Cardinal, later Pope Pius XII, consecrated his protégé titular Bishop of Sila in St. Peter's to qualify him for another return to Boston as auxiliary to Cardinal O'Connell, in 1932.

Seven years later, Bishop Spellman had been plucked out of the city once again to become Archbishop of New York, as the successor to Patrick Cardinal Hayes.

There long has been speculation over just how friendly relations were between the politically astute Spellman and the roughhewn Cushing from the time they were fellow boarders at the cathedral rectory until each moved up into the hierarchy. Some observers have noted a distinct lack of warmth between the two men. Whether this chilliness actually exists and if it does what caused it is a question the answer to which remains with the two men.

In any event, regardless of Spellman's connections in the Vatican, Cushing's abilities in the Society for the Propagation of the Faith were rewarded. On April 1, 1939, Cardinal O'Connell announced that Father Cushing had been raised to the rank of domestic prelate, with the title of Right Reverend Monsignor. His promotion was among the early acts of Pope Pius XII, Francis Spellman's mentor in Rome.

An observer reported that Father Cushing received the news in his office in Franklin Street. He casually made the minor change of adding red piping to his neck apparel, glanced around at his staff, said, "That takes care of that," and went back to work.

But two months later, the then aging Cardinal O'Connell issued a statement asserting, "I am very happy to announce I have received word today from the Papal Secretary of State that the Holy Father, at my request, has named the Right Rev. R. J. Cushing as Auxiliary Bishop of Boston."

Monsignor Cushing's acceptance of the honor was not as pat as the official statement indicated. It took him three days to make up his mind whether or not to accept it. He has given several versions of what took place between him and the old Cardinal. One of them goes this way:

"I don't want this thing, your Eminence," said Cushing when he learned of O'Connell's move. "It just doesn't appeal to me. I'm perfectly happy where I am. There must be a number of priests who want to be bishops. They can have it, I just don't want it."

The aging prelate, then eighty years old and in failing health, may have recalled the scene eighteen years earlier when the same priest, then a brash young whippersnapper, had balked at university study to become a teacher.

"Well," he said finally, "you had better think it over for a couple of days."

"I was back in two days," Cushing later recalled, "and I said, 'I don't want it; it doesn't appeal to me, and the only way I'll take it is if your Eminence makes it a command.' "

The old Cardinal shook his head like a bulldog and thundered, "You take it!"

"So, I took it!" Richard Cushing said.

Cardinal O'Connell was still so disturbed by his protégé's inferred insubordination that he arbitrarily set June 29, 1939, as the date of Cushing's consecration as auxiliary bishop, giving the forty-four-year-old priest no time to issue formal invitations. Still, more than 4,000 persons were on hand, either inside the Cathedral of the Holy Cross or on the streets outside. In a front seat of honor was eighty-one-year-old Mary Dahill Cushing, a widow since Patrick had died of pneumonia in 1922. She herself had only a year of life left, and this ceremony was one of its crowning moments.

Cardinal O'Connell officiated. And Archbishop Spellman of New York looked on from a seat in the sanctuary. As the Cardinal posed categorical questions on the monsignor's belief in matters of faith, and especially that of the Incarnation, a hush fell over the crowded cathedral.

The bishop-elect answered each question firmly, arising from a faldstool on which he had been seated. Then, he pledged his allegiance to Pope Pius XII and the Roman Catholic Church.

With the close of the examination, Cardinal O'Connell turned toward the main altar and began the celebration of a low mass. Bishop-elect Cushing, assisted by the two co-consecrators, advanced to a small, temporary alter at the Epistle side and simultaneously began offering a low mass, intended to emphasize the need for humility in the hour of exaltation.

The new bishop was somberly vested for the moment in contrast to the brilliant red capes of the Cardinal and the assisting bishops and the red vestments of the eleven monsignori who were seated in the sanctuary.

The bishop-elect continued with the mass until the offertory, when he advanced with slow, deliberate steps to the center of the sanctuary for the 15-minute ritual that would make him a bishop in fact.

Cardinal O'Connell intoned, "Lord have mercy upon us," to signal a choir of priests to chant the Litany of the Saints. A murmur arose from the congregation as Richard Cushing prostrated himself before the main altar.

As the voices of the choir rose with the chant, the music from time to time was shattered by the rattle and roar of passing Elevated trains above Washington Street. At the conclusion of the litany, Cardinal O'Connell, holding his crozier in his left hand, turned to Monsignor Cushing and repeated the first line of the litany, "that thou wouldst vouchsafe to bless this elect here present." And the choir responded, "We beseech thee, hear us."

With the aid of the two assisting bishops, the Cardinal then took the open book of the Gospels and without a word placed it on the shoulders of the bishop-elect so that the printed pages touched his neck.

Following this ceremony, Cardinal O'Connell and the co-consecrators touched the head of the bishop-elect with their hands as the Cardinal, in a loud voice that carried through the cathedral, called, "Receive the Holy Ghost!"

Laying aside his miter, the Cardinal continued, "Be propitious, O Lord, to our supplications, and inclining the horn of sacerdotal grace above this thy servant, Richard Cushing, pour out through him the power of thy blessing. Through our Lord, Jesus Christ, who liveth and reigneth with thee in the unity of the Holy Ghost, God."

Thereupon, Cardinal O'Connell anointed the new bishop's forehead with holy chrism and made the sign of the cross over his head three times, repeating the blessing, "In the name of the Father and of the Son and of the Holy Ghost, Amen," each time.

While the choir chanted an antiphon, the Cardinal and his assistants knelt. At the conclusion, Bishop Cushing arose and walked down the five steps of the main altar, this time to resume his mass with the Cardinal.

Pausing only long enough to receive the kiss of peace from the Cardinal and two brother bishops, the new prelate moved on to complete the mass.

A few moments later, the ceremony of investiture was

completed and Bishop Cushing walked from his position at the foot of the altar to a faldstool at the center that had been used, up to that moment, by the Cardinal. There, arrayed in his own red robes and holding in his right hand, for the first time, the crozier that symbolized his rank as shepherd of one flock, the new bishop looked out on his congregation.

With steady step, Bishop Cushing then walked from the altar to the front pew to bestow his first blessing as a bishop on his mother, whose eyes were streaming with tears of joy.

CHAPTER IV

Pastoral Bishop

WHEN Richard Cushing assumed his duties as auxiliary bishop, he found himself wearing three hats. In addition to being a stand-in for the aging Cardinal O'Connell, he continued as director of the Society for the Propagation of the Faith and also succeeded the departing Francis Spellman as pastor of Sacred Heart Parish in suburban Newton.

Newton was a wealthy community, contiguous to Boston, to which a new generation of sophisticated Catholics had moved with a general surge into suburbia. They had become contractors, insurance executives and bankers, and they could afford to hire a succeeding wave of immigrants, the Italians, to tend their wide lawns and evergreen shrubs. They were generous givers to the Church, and in their way as devout as the dock workers and streetcar motormen from South Boston.

Many of the women attended mass daily, and a few men if they had not become commuters to Boston; but they all were in church on Sunday and on holy days of obligation. They accepted the dogmas of Rome, as expounded by their pastors, but some of them were beginning to apply a dash of personal salt to some areas of theology. And as they gained in economic stature there was an increasing tendency to practice birth control.

But the overshadowing influence of William Cardinal O'Connell was still a powerful factor in the archdiocese, and in matters of morals and theology, even in sophisticated parishes like Sacred Heart, the voice of the Church was heard, loud and clear. And the forty-four-year-old bishop carried out the duties of defending the faith uncompromisingly, as a loyal aide of the ranking prelate.

The Roman Catholic Church had become a mighty force in the community. It had, indeed, emerged from the catacombs. Pastors were reminded that there was only one Catholic Church and that it did not need to acknowledge the distinction of being Roman Catholic. The term Protestant was being replaced by the designation "non-Catholic."

But for all that, the aging establishment was conservative, slow-moving and cumbersome. It had great potential as a political force, but little flair for igniting its energy, except in moral matters. The Cardinal could, and did, choke off a move to legalize a state lottery as a source of revenue. And he was credited with lending a hand in defeating James M. Curley, in one of his final campaigns for mayor of Boston, in favor of a promising young Irish politician, Maurice J. Tobin. Although the Church had a concern for morality in public office, the establishment lacked the initiative to keep a tight rein on some of the young Irishmen who were moving into control of the Democratic Party in Massachusetts. And a young bishop was not in position to intrude himself too deeply into matters of public policy.

In that year of 1939, Bishop Cushing was a lantern-jawed

man of supple strength that showed in his erect carriage, the healthy glow in his face and a figure that suggested a loose-limbed athlete. However he might relax among the few intimates of the old days in South Boston, the prelate turned a stern but serene face toward the world.

But the young people of his parish soon learned that he had a warmer side to him. Sacred Heart was wealthy enough to have a parochial school, and although the new pastor, accustomed to the rigid training of the Jesuits at Boston College, backed the Sisters to the limit on matters of discipline and insisted that classrooms were for learning, pupils at the school soon realized that their pastor had a soft spot for children.

At parish fetes Bishop Cushing delighted in boosting youngsters onto Ferris wheels or stuffing them with ice cream and soda pop until their mothers were horrified. And when he was not busy taking a personal hand in the activities he was taking colored pictures to show later.

He donated a jukebox to the school. He insisted on calling it a nickelodeon, and he did not object to jazz. One afternoon the Sisters heard a burst of music from a corridor while classes were still in session. Two girls were sent from one room to "tell that boy to leave that thing alone."

The girls came back giggling. The player of the jukebox was Bishop Cushing. Later one of the Sisters asked, "What was he playing, swing?"

"Well, Sister, it wasn't Bach," one of the girls said.

With small children he was completely at ease. Arriving one morning at a parish church for a confirmation service he spotted a tiny youngster standing on the sidewalk unabashedly interested in the red-robed figure.

"Hello, sonny," the bishop said. "What's your name?"

41

"Donnie," the child replied. "What's yours?"

"Richard," the bishop said, throwing back his head and roaring as he entered the church.

The confirmation of the young was an important part of his duties, the rite being reserved in liturgical churches to clergymen with the rank of bishop. Although he adhered to the ritualistic requirements of the Church, Bishop Cushing enjoyed conducting an informal examination of the candidates, either striding back and forth before the altar or coming down into the nave of the church.

One morning, he pointed a question at the end of a stern finger at a thirteen-year-old boy, who, awestruck, gave a wholly wrong answer.

"Why, that's marvelous!" exclaimed the bishop, swiftly turning to someone else.

"How many wish to be priests?" he asked one congregation.

As dozens of hands shot up, a baby somewhere in the congregation began to wail.

"That's wonderful!" roared the bishop. "And I'm sure that, some day, you'll make a fine priest, too!"

Following confirmations, as he did after ordinations, Bishop Cushing would walk down the aisle in procession, offering his ring to be kissed by any child he happened to spot near the end of a row. An adult, attempting to lean down to pay his respects, might find the ring suddenly jerked away in favor of a child.

In a procession one morning, the newly confirmed class led the way and then parted ranks outside to permit the prelate to walk between them to his waiting car. But suddenly there was no bishop. Back in the church, Bishop Cushing was found helping a small boy adjust his camera. Patiently, the bishop posed until the picture was taken.

"He's only a little shaver, now," the bishop commented, "but he'll remember this day when he grows up."

On another morning, the bishop delayed his departure from one parish in order to wait for a boy to sprint home for a camera he had forgotten to bring in the excitement of being confirmed.

Always forbearing with children, Cushing seems particularly amused and interested by children with cameras, and he has never been reluctant to let them take pictures of him. Years later, after he had become archbishop, he was meditating in the sacristy of the cathedral before celebrating high mass. The silence was shattered by the unholy clatter of feet, and a small boy charged in. He was twelve-year-old Patrick Luongo, with a camera.

Deacons, subdeacons, acolytes and a throng of young seminarians looked aghast. For something like this, penance could go on until the boy was a grown man. Then, the archbishop spoke:

"Whom do you represent—the *Pilot?*"

The boy, suddenly realizing his situation, swallowed silently.

The archbishop smiled and turned to a nearby priest, commenting, "Maybe he's from the South Boston *Gazette.*"

As the prelate was assisted in donning his ermine cape and long ceremonial train, the boy clicked away. Finally, Archbishop Cushing nodded that it was time to move into the sanctuary.

Patrick Luongo turned and ran out, his new Easter shoes clattering louder than before.

During the war, the pressure of diocesan duties sometimes made it necessary to hold a confirmation service whenever a mutually agreeable time could be arranged. An adult woman convert, appearing one morning at an 8:30

A.M. mass, to be accepted into the Catholic faith, received the laying on of hands. The bishop glanced at her name on a card presented him and continued with the service without further ado.

Ten months later, the same woman appeared as the sponsor for 500 youngsters at a confirmation service in the same parish. As the bishop made his customary way down the aisle, he noted the woman kneeling with the others.

Offering her his ring, Bishop Cushing whispered, "You're getting the trimmings today you missed when you were confirmed."

A little more than two years after Cushing became bishop, still carrying on many of his duties in the Propagation office, the world was plunged into war again, for the second time in his life. Cushing immediately stepped up his fund-raising activities for missions in the Pacific and broadened his interests to include those of his parishioners who were in the armed services. He sent silver rosaries to the ones who were leaving home for the service; and when the War Department sent telegrams saying "The Secretary of War regrets . . ." Bishop Cushing personally celebrated the requiem mass for the dead to comfort the grieving family.

He had made it a practice to send out pastoral letters to children shortly before the first Friday of each month, to remind them of their duty to attend mass. During the war he used these letters to buoy up the spirits of the young. In one of them he wrote:

> Surely, Mary will answer your prayer. You have been doing everything that little children can do to help your country in this present crisis. You have been performing your duties at home, at school and at church. You have given your "mighty mites" for stamps and bonds. At your

communion of Friday and at daily mass pray, pray, pray for peace.

Next to the prayers that the priest offers at the holy sacrifice of the mass, there are no prayers more powerful than those that fall from the lips of God's children.

The parochial school benefited by the pastor's acquaintance with missionaries during the wartime period. He arranged for the visit of a Chinese bishop who had been forced to flee the fighting in the South Pacific. And an American chaplain, furloughed home from the front, was invited in to talk with the children about where their nickels and dimes for missions had gone to help other children in the Far East. There was a reading, too, of the letter of an American Navy commander named Shea to his son a few weeks before he plunged to his own death sinking a Japanese warship.

Onerous as wartime duties were, Bishop Cushing showed a characteristic concern for his curates who had to bear the burden of many pastoral duties. He would dismiss them at noon on Thanksgiving Day or after the last mass on Christmas morning so that they could have dinner with their own families. And while he kept up cordial relations with his brother and sisters, the bishop insisted that they live their own lives without regard to the position he held.

Along with the heavy responsibilities of his parish and his duties as a bishop, Cushing continued to direct the office of the Society for the Propagation of the Faith. He was there one winter morning when a missionary from the South dropped in. The visiting priest was shivering, explaining that the warm climate in which he was used to working had thinned his blood. When he left, despite his protests, he was wearing the warm overcoat of the auxiliary Bishop of Boston.

Missionary work had always been Cushing's chief interest and during the war he exerted extraordinary efforts in its behalf. On learning of the bayoneting of a priest in the South Pacific, he delivered eleven speeches in twelve hours at the Mission church in Roxbury, raising $15,000 for missionary work in the Solomon Islands from audiences totaling more than 20,000.

Despite his heavy schedule, Bishop Cushing made himself available day and night. A nun who knew him said, commenting on his work, "The greater the need of a person, the more eager he is to respond to a plea for assistance. He is impartial, but if he favors any particular group, they are the needy and those in sorrow. He never has refused to help anyone whose need is an honest one."

His favors went beyond the members of his own diocese. On one occasion the minister of a small Protestant congregation came to ask the bishop if he could spare some folding chairs. Bishop Cushing thought a moment, then said, "Well, if you can round up half a dozen husky men to do the unloading, I think I can find a truck to deliver them about 5:30 tonight."

In his downtown office the bishop showed a visitor a letter from a little girl who was a patient in the Peabody Home for Crippled Children, a nondenominational institution. "Dear Bishop Cushing," the letter read, "I am not a Catholic, but I asked my minister if I could write to you and he said I could. What I want to know is when you are coming again to give us another movie show."

Some friends of Cushing's old teacher, Father Keating, planned to present him with a golden chalice in honor of the fiftieth anniversary of his ordination. They wanted to present it to him the night before so that he could use it on the anniversary date. At the last moment someone recalled

that a chalice could not be used until it had been consecrated by a bishop. A friend of Keating's telephoned the
rectory of Sacred Heart on the chance that the bishop
might be free. He was, and he would be glad to bless the
chalice for his old teacher. Although he had a speaking engagement, Cushing paced up and down in front of the rectory until Keating's friends arrived with the chalice. They
went in, the chalice was blessed, and Cushing hurried off to
keep his engagement.

In increasing demand as a speaker at public functions
aside from religious gatherings, Bishop Cushing found himself one night in 1943 addressing the annual dinner of the
Charitable Irish in Boston. Among the guests at the head
table were Senators Leverett Saltonstall of Massachusetts
and Robert A. Taft of Ohio.

Bishop Cushing arose to speak. He looked around.

"Taft!"

A pause.

"Saltonstall!"

Another pause.

"Cushing!"

A brittle pause.

"What a ticket!"

A shattering cheer.

The bishop could be equally disarming to an audience of
women. He arrived behind time one morning at a communion breakfast.

"I am very sorry to be late, ladies, but the member of the
committee whom you sent to call for me," said the bishop
with a low bow, "wore so large a hat it blew out of the
window and I had to walk back and pick it up!"

One reason that Bishop Cushing could keep his many
engagements punctually was the devotion of his chauffeur,

Alfred C. Wasilauskas, who was his faithful aide until he died of cancer. In addition to driving Cushing's car, he performed other tasks, such as tying parcels, stamping mail and operating the movie projector at the bishop's frequent performances.

One day in 1943, when the bishop was to be present at a parochial school band competition at Boston College, word came that he would have a guest with him. Hurried preparations were made to provide an extra seat on the reviewing stand, just as the bishop's car arrived at the entrance to the field. On the back seat with the prelate was Ann Wasilauskas, the chauffeur's small daughter.

CHAPTER V

Ut Cognoscant Te

WILLIAM CARDINAL O'CONNELL died peacefully at 5:45 P.M., April 22, 1944, after four days' struggle with bronchial pneumonia. One of his last acts as spiritual sovereign of an archdiocese that had grown to embrace more than a million Roman Catholic communicants was feebly to stretch out his right hand in a blessing. Within two hours, the Most Rev. Richard J. Cushing had been appointed administrator of the archdiocese by a committee of councilors.

As bells throughout the archdiocese began to toll, the councilors made arrangements for four days of mourning, followed by a pontifical requiem mass at the cathedral. Archbishop Amleto G. Cicognani, the Apostolic Delegate of the Vatican in Washington, came up to Boston to preside. Bishop Cushing, in the eulogy, took as his text a passage from the Apocryphal book of Ecclesiasticus: "Behold a great priest who in his days pleased God and was found just; and in the time of wrath was made a reconciliation." Following a request of the Cardinal some time before his death, he was buried in a crypt of a chapel he had built on

49

the grounds of his estate several years earlier. The small mausoleum provided space for additional bodies.

The forty-eight-year-old Cushing was now in charge of the archdiocese, but only on an interim basis. The councilors might select a temporary administrator, but only the Pope could appoint a permanent ruler to set and carry out policy. As an auxiliary bishop, Cushing was merely an extension of the authority of the Cardinal. He has never given any indication that he was consulted on policy by the strong-willed O'Connell. Years later he said, "I never had anything to do with the running of the diocese. I was always on the outside, never involved in internal affairs." He has never revealed much of his relationship with the Cardinal. He has commented, "Whether he wanted me or not, I don't know, but I think he had others in mind, although he was always good to me, like a father."

As a young priest, Father Cushing had been chosen to live in the archepiscopal residence, at that time in suburban Brookline, while O'Connell was away. All he has revealed of this is that he had something to do with the death of the Cardinal's favorite dog.

"Any time the Cardinal went away, I had to stay at his house," Cushing has told audiences. "I was very husky then, I weighed about two hundred pounds and had a pompadour haircut, that led people to call me Tunney, after the world champion prize fighter. I had to be responsible for the house, including the dog. His name was Moro. I hated dogs.

"Then, there was the Irish cook. I feared her more than I did the Cardinal. She'd come up in the morning and she'd ask you what you'd like for breakfast. Well, she would have a big platter with baloney, sausages, eggs and bacon, plunk it down in front of you and say, 'Eat!' I used to feed the sausages to Moro.

"Two days before the Cardinal came back from one of his trips to Nassau, Moro died. Now, Moro meant more to his Eminence than I did, so when the dog died, I said to myself, 'I guess I'd better pack up, because I'm sure going to be shipped out to the missions.'

"When the Cardinal came home, I said, "Your Eminence, I have very sad news; Moro died.'

" 'Moro died?' the Cardinal repeated. 'He must have pined away for his master.'

"But I thought to myself, 'He pined away from those sausages,' " said Cushing.

Now, as administrator, Bishop Cushing had the responsibility of an archdiocese, a position that called for a clergyman with the rank of archbishop, at least, if not cardinal. As an archdiocese, Boston was the center of a province that included all of the New England states except Connecticut—the dioceses of Portland, Maine; Manchester, New Hampshire; Burlington, Vermont; Providence, Rhode Island; and Springfield, Worcester, and Fall River, Massachusetts; each with its own bishop, who in matters such as marriage tribunals would be subordinate to the Boston prelate, or chief bishop.

The interregnum of Bishop Cushing as acting administrator of the archdiocese proved to be relatively short. About 8 P.M., on September 28, 1944, Archbishop Cicognani telephoned from Washington to notify the prelate that he had been appointed Archbishop of Boston by Pope Pius XII. Shortly afterward, the new archbishop-elect retired for the night.

Not insensible of the responsibility that had fallen on

him, the new archbishop-elect had his secretary, Monsignor
Wright, prepare a formal statement for the wire services
when the telephone began ringing in the rectory of Sacred
Heart Church.

"My first act is to ask all to join with me in fervent prayers to Almighty God," said the Archbishop's
statement. "May He inspire and strengthen me. May He
grant me light to know His will, guide me to do His work,
grace to speed His holy message of faith and love and salvation everywhere at home and throughout the sorely tried
missions."

For the first time, the high school dropout from South
Boston was about to become his own man. The heavy hand
of the past had been lifted. But there were some formalities
first. He had to be installed archbishop of the see in proper
ceremonies. And technically, he could not assume full title
as Primate of New England until he had been invested with
the pallium that was the badge of his office.

The pallium is a circular band of white wool, about two
inches wide, that is worn about the neck and shoulders. It
is woven from the wool of two lambs presented annually as
a symbolic offering to the Supreme Pontiff. The lambs are
blessed on the Feast of Saint Agnes. Later, after the wool
has been woven into cloth, it is blessed again by the Pope
on the eve of the Feast of Sts. Peter and Paul.

The pallium is conceived as being the very robe given in
apostolic times by Peter to a fellow worker in the ministry
of the Christian Church. In the prayer accompanying its
bestowal, the pallium is described as a robe taken from the
body of Peter, the first Pope.

Occasionally, the pallium is bestowed in person by the
Pope. But in the fall of 1944 war raged in the air and on
the seas between Boston and Rome and a pilgrimage to

Washington, D.C. Richard Cardinal Cushing, Archbishop of Boston, asks God's blessing for John F. Kennedy as the nation's 35th President. Cardinal Cushing delivered the invocation at the inauguration ceremonies. A Greek Orthodox prelate, a Protestant minister and a Jewish rabbi followed the Cardinal in offering prayers on behalf of the new President. *Courtesy Religious News Service*

Richard James Cushing on graduation from Oliver Hazard Perry Grammar School, South Boston.
Courtesy the Boston Globe

The Rev. Richard J. Cushing, ordination picture, 1921. *Courtesy the Boston Globe*

Mary Dahill Cushing with picture of her son, Bishop Richard J. Cushing. *Courtesy the Boston Globe*

Proud parents at christening. Sen. and Mrs. John Kennedy appear as proud parents as Mrs. Kennedy holds their infant daughter Caroline, after christening ceremony in St. Patrick's Cathedral in New York. At right is Boston's Archbishop Richard Cushing who performed the ceremony of Baptism.

Cardinal Cushing leads a chorus of friends. *Courtesy the Boston Herald*

Cardinal Cushing with
Dick Radatz, Red Sox relief
pitcher, at Fenway Park.

Archbishop Cushing and
friend, kissing his ring.
Courtesy the Boston Globe

Cardinal Cushing of Boston, left, with Cardinal Francis J. Spellman of New York. *Courtesy the Boston Herald*

Cardinal and nuns on roller coaster at Nantasket, Mass., during an outing. *Courtesy The Pilot*

Cardinal Cushing with exceptional children, at Boston airport en route to Lourdes. *Courtesy The Pilot*

the Holy City was out of the question. Under the circumstances, a pallium eventually was sent to the United States, where it was bestowed in the name of the Pope by Archbishop Spellman of New York in Boston's Holy Cross Cathedral on April 7, 1946.

The formal installation, however, could be held. And on November 8, 1944, Archbishop Cicognani made another trip from Washington to preside.

In assuming his new station, Archbishop Cushing took for his motto *Ut Cognoscant Te,* the Latin phrase for "that they may know thee." It became part of his ecclesiastical coat of arms.

The day of the installation was bitter cold. But several hundreds stood outside of the cathedral to listen to the ceremonies over a loudspeaker system. In addition, the service was carried by radio to other hundreds of thousands. The Rev. Michael J. Ahern, S. J., of Weston College, stood by a microphone in a small enclosure at the right of the altar and translated into English all of the Latin prayers and chants.

The two-hour ceremony was a scene of liturgical splendor that opened with a procession from the rectory to the main entrance of the cathedral, despite the biting wind.

As the procession flowed down the center aisle of the edifice and spread across into the sanctuary and first rows, Archbishop Cicognani ascended a special throne erected for him at the Epistle, or right, side of the altar. The new archbishop seated himself on a faldstool on the same side.

The archepiscopal throne at the left, the "cathedra" of the archdiocese, remained vacant at the beginning of the ceremony.

The chancellor of the archdiocese, Monsignor Jeremiah Minihan, read the decree of appointment and installation.

A chanting of liturgical prayers, with appropriate antiphons, versicles and responses, set the stage for the act of installation.

The apostolic delegate descended from his throne and escorted the new archbishop to the Gospel side where he presented to him a golden crozier, the pastoral staff of authority. That done, the See of Boston again had an archbishop.

Moving to the center of the altar, the new prelate imparted his first blessing as archbishop on the congregation. The St. John's Seminary choir, which only a few months before had chanted prayers for a dead cardinal, now lifted its voices in the *Te Deum Laudamus,* a fifth-century hymn, translated, "We Praise Thee, O Lord."

During the singing of the hymn, the officials of the diocese and priests in charge of diocesan bureaus approached the throne in the name of all of the clergy to renew a promise of loyalty and obedience, given first at ordination, and now repeated to the new ranking prelate of the archdiocese.

The new archbishop turned to his congregation and said, "To Almighty God I consecrate all that I have and all that I am, for His glory, for my own sanctification and for the welfare of the souls entrusted to my care.

"Pray for me," he went on, "not that I may attain the heights of learning nor the pinnacles of visible success, but that I may be saturated with, and help others achieve, that spirituality which flows from the knowledge and love of God."

In an installation sermon that followed a pontifical mass, Bishop Francis P. Keough of Providence asserted that "rarely in the history of our country has the elevation of a prelate to such a high office been more sincerely and universally welcomed than in the case of this archbishop."

At the close of the ceremony, the new archbishop repeatedly blessed those whom he passed on the way down the aisle. Outside, again ignoring the cold, he blessed those who had waited for a glimpse of him.

The following day, with most of his personal belongings in two suitcases, the Most Rev. Richard James Cushing, archbishop of one of the largest sees in the Roman Catholic Church, completed the journey from a wooden, cold-water tenement in South Boston to a stone mansion on a hill in Brighton, at the western edge of the city.

The mansion had been constructed under the direction of Cardinal O'Connell. It overlooked St. John's Seminary. And on an adjacent hilltop to the southwest stood the new buildings of Boston College, the old day school that had started in the South End, and had been rescued from mediocrity by the old alumnus-cardinal.

Although the mansion was familiar to the new prelate, through frequent visits to report to the Cardinal, he viewed it the first day as archbishop with new eyes. He confided to friends that the long, marble hallways had always reminded him of bowling alleys.

The Cardinal's valet and a retinue of house servants were dismissed. The new prelate could dress and serve himself. Anything extra could be provided by Al Wasilauskas, his chauffeur.

Three expensive limousines in the garage were disposed of and a more moderately priced sedan replaced them. More often than not, the new archbishop would beg rides home from friends.

A group of nuns was assigned to keep house. Later, after

he became Cardinal himself, Richard Cushing told an audience, "For twenty years I have lived in the archbishop's house of this diocese and in those twenty years I have never been above the second floor of that house.

"The good nuns who staff the house live on the third floor and I have never dared penetrate the third floor. I think the Holy Ghost Himself would not get up there."

As he strolled through the residence, examining the rare paintings, furniture and other works of art, the new archbishop thought of them in terms of how much they would bring at auction to finance seminary tuition for promising young men.

Gradually, but occasionally rapidly, through the years most of the treasures have gone. Even a long circular mahogany table in a reception room where the Cardinal customarily holds press conferences and greets routine visitors has been replaced by a more modest piece of furniture.

Filing cabinets, mimeographing machines, typewriters and other office equipment were installed in several rooms downstairs. Two experienced women secretaries of the Office for the Propagation of the Faith days were requisitioned for duty at the Archbishop's residence. He knew what they could do and they came as close as any human beings could to sensing what he probably would do. The Archbishop, for example, might walk out of the room in the midst of dictation to answer the telephone in person, but on his return he would take up the thread of dictation without a hitch.

When he first established residence in the mansion Archbishop Cushing ordered the private telephone number to be changed to a listed number. Subsequently, he was forced to back down. The line never seemed to stop ringing.

"I don't mind it so much in the daytime," he told his staff, "but I found out the hard way how a fireman feels at three in the morning."

Having aired out the fustiness from the archepiscopal residence, Archbishop Cushing swung into action on the archdiocese at large. He had visited every parish, mission and institution across the five counties as a fund-raising priest and auxiliary bishop, so Richard Cushing knew better than anyone else the gigantic task of rehabilitation and new construction that faced him and his flock.

And while the sweep of his plans staggered the chancery, Archbishop Cushing had ideas of his own for streamlining donations. And he knew the value of the telephone as an instrument for calling up more affluent Catholics and cajoling and demanding they dig down for the good causes.

Under the conservative administration of Cardinal O'Connell, in an era of lower prices, wages and taxes, bequests, gifts and occasional drives were enough to carry the load. But with those sources dried up through attrition by death and by the drive of the war, Archbishop Cushing turned to the financial techniques of agencies like the Red Feather and Red Cross.

Pledge cards held a record of commitments to contribute specified sums, no matter how little, each year. The solid financial base for these contributions were guilds, representing a host of businesses and professions. For example, the St. Caritas Guild, made up of members of the alcoholic beverages industry, still raises upwards of $50,000 a year.

Historically, guilds were established for obtaining and maintaining the privilege of carrying on a trade. In England, around 925 A.D., they developed into religious organizations with a corporate responsibility for the good conduct of their members and their mutual liability to the church.

Although the religious and social guilds were suppressed at the Reformation, the trade guilds survived as corporations and companies, and were the forerunners of labor unions. In modern times, in the Boston archdiocese, new guilds were formed by professional and business men as part of Catholic Action, urged by Pope Pius XI to act so that "all are harmonious in a convergent manner dependent upon ecclesiastical authority."

Physicians, under St. Luke's Guild, and dentists, under St. Apollonia's, not only raise funds for the archdiocese but they also travel around the archdiocese administering care to the underprivileged.

Other guilds include St. Michael's for communication workers; St. Agatha's for nurses; St. Ives' for lawyers, St. Francis de Sales' for journalists, and St. Joseph's for all workers.

In addition, as archbishop and later as cardinal, Richard Cushing has brought in entertainment headlinders like Dennis Day, Bob Hope, Jimmy Durante, Fred Waring, Perry Como and Jerry Colonna to Boston for special fundraising events.

At present donations to the Cardinal's personal charity fund amount to more than $16,000 a day. Many of them are small contributions from individuals; obviously Cushing has means to raise larger sums when necessary. Each donation, as well as every other piece of mail that comes into the archdiocesan offices, and there are hundreds daily, is acknowledged by the Cardinal personally within forty-eight hours. Two full-time secretaries are assisted by several part-time workers who come in for a few hours each week.

Cushing's secretaries know his style so well that he has only to indicate how each letter should be answered; but the signature is in his own hand and usually includes a scrawled "Forever grateful" besides.

Fully aware of the power of propaganda, Archbishop Cushing turned the weekly *Pilot* into a vigorous news organ, instead of a personal mouthpiece for the head of the see, as it was under Cardinal O'Connell. Catholics of the old Cardinal's day recall that the *Pilot* came wrapped in a sickly-looking pink paper and generally remained wrapped until it was used to start a kitchen fire.

Three successive editors, Fathers John S. Sexton and Francis P. Moran and Monsignor Lally, have had freer reign to turn the paper into something that is widely read, not as a duty, but as a voice to be heard and heeded.

As a result, the *Pilot* often has taken a lively part in public debates and is carefully read on Boston city desks for its editorials and its news. As an adjunct of the *Pilot,* the Archbishop also activated a diocesan news bureau, headed by a layman, George E. Ryan. The bureau turns out texts of speeches by the prelate when he particularly wants them publicized, as well as news of the archdiocese.

Besides the recitation of the Rosary thrice daily over commercial radio stations, the archdiocese has established its own television station. Christmas Eve mass, with the Archbishop presiding, was telecast locally in 1949. And the following year, it was nationally televised on the National Broadcasting System network.

Aware that as people began moving out of Boston to the suburbs it would become increasingly difficult for them to live up to their weekday religious obligations and still catch the 7:15 into town, Archbishop Cushing began to establish a series of workers' chapels, where they could drop in for confession or mass or meditation in the heart of the business district.

Such chapels were set up at the Logan International Airport, at the South Station railroad terminal, at the State Fish Pier, in shopping centers. And one of the largest, St. Anthony's, was erected in recent years on Arch Street, strategically situated between the shopping and financial districts.

A shrine on Arch Street has long been in existence. The Cardinal sometimes tells audiences of a day when he was a young priest and was called by the shrine office to go to the first-aid room of a downtown department store. An elderly man had been stricken, apparently with a heart attack.

The young priest looked at the man on the cot and at the attending store nurse and commented that he didn't think the man was dying. But, dutifully, he leaned over the man and asked, "Do you believe in the Father, Son and Holy Ghost?"

The man opened one eye, looked at the nurse and mumbled, "I'm dying and he's asking me riddles!"

In one version, Richard Cushing sometimes asserts that with that, the man got up and walked out, whereupon the priest turned to the nurse, thumped his chest and exclaimed, "Look at the power of the man!"

But, in bringing the Church to the people, the Archbishop also invited many orders of priests, brothers and nuns to establish new foundations or further existing ones, particularly in social work and missionary fields.

Pursuing a policy of completing payment for each building under construction so that it would be free of debt when it was opened for service, the Cardinal has spent upwards of $250,000,000 on schools, hospitals and other institutions.

A few months after his installation, the Archbishop opened St. Francis' Refuge, where indigent men, some of them human derelicts, of all ages are given a substantial meal a day.

But two institutions particularly close to the prelate are Nazareth, a boarding school for temporarily homeless children, and St. Coletta's, an institution for mentally and physically deficient children.

In referring to Nazareth, the Cardinal always avoids the term "destitute," apparently on the theory that as long as people will support the institution, the children there will not be destitute.

Social services that endeavor to keep families intact by remedying home and personal situations are centered at Nazareth. These services include the furnishing of capable women to take over households in emergencies and bus transportation to gather children for whom eight or ten hours of care daily are necessary.

The 160 children at St. Coletta's are referred to by the Archbishop as "exceptional" rather than retarded children. He sometimes calls them "the least of the brethren," or "the forever children."

In any event, the prelate made it clear some years ago that rather than be buried in the crypt of the chapel at his residence, he wants to lie in a cemetery at St. Coletta's near the children.

CHAPTER VI

Heretics and Fanatics

THE end of the war brought no letup in the activities of the Archbishop. As auxiliary to the ailing Cardinal O'Connell, Richard Cushing's administrative duties had been heavy; and the war had entailed additional efforts on behalf of the missions. Under O'Connell, the affairs of the diocese had lumbered along in a traditional stately way. Now Archbishop Cushing was modernizing procedures to meet the needs of an increased flock and a swifter pace of life. In addition he was responsible for policy and for representing the attitudes of the Church in an entirely different kind of world.

The defeat of Nazism, and the consolidation of Communism in eastern Europe drastically altered the status not merely of the Roman Catholic Church but of all of Western Christendom. Far from uniting the victorious powers in religious and secular freedom of thought and action, the end of the war brought new outbursts of religious persecution in Europe and bigotry and anticlericalism in America. And within the Church itself there appeared new evidence of ancient schisms that in part was to inspire the Second

Vatican Council, the Church's great effort to heal the differences among all Christian denominations as well as to broaden its own dogmas.

Boston, with its Protestant cultural tradition and its large Roman Catholic population and economic and political power, has had a significant share of conflicts that reflect the worldwide currents of change. Although the spirit of the Nativist movement of the 1830s and 1840s and the Know Nothing movement of the 1850s has disappeared, there are still vestiges of the American Protective Association feelings of the 1890s. A current Catholic guidebook to Boston reminds readers that in 1834 a mob of bigots attacked and burned an Ursuline Convent in the old Charlestown district.

This kind of ignorant prejudice seems to have vanished; but nevertheless bigotry still appears, outside the circles of Church and within it, and in the past two decades some notable instances of it have occurred in Boston. To outlanders they may seem merely domestic and local problems, isolated cases of prejudice in a particular community. But in the perspective of time and of the declarations of three sessions of a Vatican Council, they have clearly been symptoms of a broader upheaval, readjustment and reformation of religious attitudes.

As Archbishop, Richard Cushing has had to become the voice of the Church of these matters; the task of reconciling conflicts within his own archdiocese has been an enormous and a precarious one, since he has had to establish a firm line for his own parishioners, keep peace in a community where religious antagonisms have flourished for a century and a half, and take his part in forging the ecumenical policies of the whole Roman Catholic Church.

As a Roman Catholic he has always taken a firm stand

against the atheistic philosophy of Communism. To critics on the national scene his premature and uninformed endorsement of the John Birch Society and his refusal to condemn the political policies of the late Senator McCarthy momentarily marked him as an extreme right-winger. On the other hand, his views on matters of religious and racial tolerance bear witness to the ecumenical spirit that made him a powerful progressive influence at the Vatican Council and that has always been evident to thoughtful Bostonians of all faiths, even though on specific issues he has occasionally come into sharp conflict with Protestant and Jewish leaders.

Differences of opinion and even open antagonism with members of other faiths, and the defense of Christian faith against atheistic political power have always been routine trials for any prelate. Much harder to contemplate, endure, and resolve are schisms within the Church itself.

The controversy over the religious views of the Jesuit teacher and writer Father Feeney was an intrachurch matter and although it received general publicity in Boston, it was entirely up to the Church to determine the extent of Father Feeney's insubordination and the proper way of dealing with it. The case attracted notice not only because of Father Feeney's reputation as a writer and speaker but also because of his apparent determination to force action both from the archdiocese and the Holy See. Archbishop Cushing's treatment of the case was restrained and deliberate. He dealt with it as a matter that concerned only the authority of the Church; yet he could not have helped seeing that its central issue involved the whole relationship of Catholics with non-Catholics; and in fact even after the Church had formally made its pronouncement on the Feeneyites, they were openly attacking non-Catholics, particularly Jews and Protestants.

To some Catholics, despite the finality of the Church's ruling, the case has never been fully resolved. It concerned the doctrine of salvation, one of the underlying issues of the Second Vatican Council. The crux of the matter was the question, "Is there salvation outside the [Roman] Catholic Church?"

It is a dogma that has vexed theologians and scholars for centuries. The old school has held that salvation is impossible without submission to the Pope and to the tenets of Rome. But within the last century, as the winds of change have begun to eddy through the Church, there has been a growing feeling that more liberal interpretation of the belief would indicate that those of good intentions or faith might be considered eligible for ultimate salvation.

And while theologians and scholars might discuss the matter dispassionately in the isolated climate of the ivory tower, no such climate existed in the Boston archdiocese in 1949.

The key figures of the Feeney controversy were four lay teachers in Boston College and its affiliated high school, and the Rev. Leonard Feeney, S.J., the spiritual director of the St. Benedict Center, a Catholic teaching house near Harvard Square, Cambridge.

Father Feeney, then fifty-two years old, was a short man with a dimpled face and an enthusiastic manner of speaking. He was born in Lynn of a family that included two other priests, the Rev. Thomas B. Feeney, S.J., and the Rev. John Feeney.

After being graduated with honors from Boston College, Father Leonard Feeney attended the Jesuit House in Weston, Massachusetts, and later studied at Oxford University. He taught English in the Boston College graduate school in the 1930s.

During his student days, preparing for the exacting duties of a Jesuit, Father Feeney's writings of poetry and prose, especially an article scoring companionate marriage, brought him wide notice in the Church.

He later came to be known outside for his sense of humor as well as for his literary efforts. One of his friends was the late Alfred E. Smith, whose Presidential candidacy in 1928 was enlivened in the nation's press by a letter written by Father Feeney on the politician's famous brown derby.

For a number of years, Father Feeney was one of the most prolific contributors to *America*, a Jesuit weekly publication. He was sought after as a speaker in Boston and in New York.

The St. Benedict Center was founded in 1942 by Catholics at Harvard as a somewhat more sophisticated version of the Newman Clubs for Catholic students at other universities. In 1949 Father Feeney was assigned to it. Until that time the center offered lectures and discussion groups on Catholic questions, as part of the Catholic Action Movement instituted by Pope Pius X. Members were expected to be guided by Catholic principles in politics, recreation, and their daily lives. But soon after Father Feeney took charge, the center became a full-dress educational institution, teaching Greek, church history, philosophy, literature and hagiography, a study of the lives of saints. Father Feeney also titillated the students with his erudition and histrionics. He enjoyed doing such impersonations as President Roosevelt talking about the state of the Church or Katherine Hepburn broadcasting a prizefight. The state board of collegiate authority qualified the center for training under the G.I. Bill of Rights for the education of war veterans.

The center claimed to have made more than 200 converts to Catholicism and said that about 100 members and guests had become priests or nuns. An average of 250 students attended courses at various times, fifty of them full time.

Within the center and its parent institution, Boston College, there had been dissension for several months in 1949 over the doctrines and teaching methods of four teachers: Dr. Fakhri Maluf, an assistant professor of philosophy; James R. Walsh, an instructor in philosophy; Charles Ewaskio, an assistant professor of physics; and David R. Supple, a teacher of German at the high school. The upshot was that the teachers accused the Very Rev. William L. Keleher, S.J., president of Boston College, of heresy on three counts. They charged that he permitted his students to be taught (1) that there might be salvation outside the Catholic Church, (2) that a man might be saved though he did not hold that the Catholic Church was supreme among churches, and (3) that he might be saved without submission to the Pope.

The controversy spilled over into the public domain on April 14, when Father Keleher issued a statement saying that the four had been warned to cease their own contrary teaching or leave the faculty.

Father Keleher's formal statement read:

> These gentlemen in question were under contract at Boston College to teach philosophy and physics. They had been cautioned by me and others in authority here to stay within their own fields and leave theology to those who were adequately and competently prepared.
>
> They continued to speak in class and out of class on

matters contrary to the teaching of the Catholic Church, ideas leading to bigotry and intolerance.

Their doctrine is erroneous and as such could not be tolerated at Boston College. They were informed that they must cease such teaching or leave the faculty.

A college official explained that Father Keleher's stand on salvation was spelled out in the Baltimore Catechism, used by the Church for basic instruction of children and of converts. It was promulgated at a national session known as the Third Plenary Council of Baltimore in 1884.

The nub of the situation, in the catechism, was that "he who knows the church to be the true church and remains out of it cannot be saved." The catechism explained that the matter of remaining out of the church "applies to men who sin against the truth." But it said this did not apply to "men of good faith that belong to the soul of the church." The catechism defined the soul of the church as comprising "all that possess God's good grace, even if they are not members."

Two days after the dismissal, Father Feeney publicly came to the defense of the four men, all of whom taught part-time at the St. Benedict Center. The priest not only praised all four as teachers but he also asserted, "I was very much surprised to learn from newspaper reports that Father Keleher had said that a profession—and where needed an explanation—of the truths of our holy faith is forbidden any Catholic teachers speaking to Catholic students at a Catholic college."

The same evening the four teachers visited Boston newspaper offices with a statement that they had been fired on the spot when they confronted Father Keleher in his office. They also revealed that they had bypassed both the college and the archdiocese by writing directly to Pope Pius XII, and predicted that the papal reaction would destroy the heresy of liberalism. Actually they had received an acknowledgment and the usual apostolic blessing from the Secretariat of State of the Vatican, but no sanction for their position.

The archdiocesan chancery kept silent, and the four teachers maintained that only the Pope could settle the matter. They had, however, complained to the provincial of the Eastern Province of the Society of Jesus that their consciences were being violated. And they professed incredulity that Father Keleher should have fired them without consulting the Archbishop.

The chancery was not long in making a statement once the discharged professors had forced the issue. On the afternoon of April 18, newspapers were notified that a statement from the Archbishop would be available at 10 P.M. It was handed out, without comment, by the Right Rev. Msgr. Walter J. Furlong, chancellor of the archdiocese.

It read:

This morning the four professors who have been publicizing their disagreement with alleged teachings at Boston College, finally called upon me. I had read in the newspapers that they had written the Holy See, the general of the Jesuits and others. I had also heard that they and a few misguided partisans had been picketing churches and otherwise scandalizing the community during the week.

Many persons had asked me for comment, but I declined to make any declaration which might make it more difficult for these members of my flock and those whom they have influenced to straighten out the problem which they have created for themselves and their friends.

Moreover, I had frequently befriended the center in Cambridge, which appears to share their views and to support their present unreasonable action; so had my assistants in the work of the archdiocese.

Now that they have finally come to me and have published to the press the fact of their visit, I am obliged to state that I deplore the action they have taken and the serious scandal which they have caused. Weighty points of dogma are not debated in headlines or made the occasion of recrimination and immoderate attack on constituted authority.

I counseled these young men to share the wisdom and the patience of the church and to respect her sane procedures in presenting the truth.

They appeared unwilling to heed this counsel, but I renew my prayer that they will come to a better understanding of the spirit in which the Catholic Church meets problems so close to the interest of souls, those of the faithful and of others alike. . . .

I regret that the young men brought into the public press the name of Father Leonard Feeney in connection with this problem. They have thus obliged me to reveal the unhappy fact that Father Feeney has been defying the orders of his legitimate superiors for more than seven months and since Jan. 1 of this year has not possessed the faculties of this archdiocese.

In the face of his present public action I am also obliged to announce that the so-called "St. Benedict Centre" is henceforth totally without ecclesiastical approbation, and attendance at it is strictly forbidden to Catholics. I make this declaration in the form of the following decree and this will be my last public comment on this painful matter.

Any further notoriety given the case will be due entirely to the ill will of others.

Decree: The Rev. Leonard Feeney, S.J., because of grave offenses against the general laws of the Catholic Church, has lost the right to perform any priestly functions, including preaching and teaching of religion.

Any Catholics who frequent St. Benedict's Centre, or who in any way take part in or assist its activities forfeit the right to receive the sacraments of penance and Holy Eucharist.

> Given at Boston, on the 18th day of April, 1949.
> (signed) RICHARD J. CUSHING
> Archbishop of Boston
> (undersigned) WALTER J. FURLONG,
> Chancellor

Father Feeney immediately fired back with a statement asserting, "The reason I am being silenced is because I believe there is no salvation outside the Catholic Church and without personal submission to our Holy Father, and Archbishop Cushing believes there is, and Bishop Wright believes there is." Bishop John J. Wright, now Bishop of Pittsburgh, then was the Auxiliary Bishop of Boston.

Although Archbishop Cushing did not specify the "grave offenses" mentioned in his statement, Father Feeney disclosed that he had been ordered out of the diocese seven months earlier because of his beliefs about salvation. The order was in fact a transfer to duties at Holy Cross College at Worcester, Massachusetts, which Father Feeney refused to accept.

Despite the Archbishop's declaring St. Benedict Center out of bounds to Catholics, Father Feeney and the directors decided to keep it open under their own auspices. They asserted that the center was "not founded by a decree of the Archbishop and will not be dissolved by such a decree."

Then, on April 22, an unofficial statement from the Vatican was carried on news service wires. It asserted that Archbishop Cushing was a "very prudent man" who must have had reasons for his action and describing Father Feeney's silencing as valid.

Referring to the Boston College case, the Vatican statement commented that "some people have exaggerated its importance. Similar disputes occur frequently. Generally, they are settled locally. The church fixed its teachings on this matter long ago."

One agency report said it presumed this to be in reference to an allocution of Pope Pius IX, issued December 9, 1854, asserting that "those who are ignorant of the true religion . . . will not be held guilty in this matter in the eyes of the Lord."

Apparently the Holy See had spoken, but the Feeneyites were not prepared to drop the matter. When by coincidence in April, 1949, the National Catholic Welfare Council in Washington, representing the American hierarchy, published a new catechism whose doctrine on salvation was the same as that of the Baltimore Catechism of 1884, the St. Benedict Center asserted that it contradicted the Church's traditional dogma on the question and asked for an ex-cathedra pronouncement from the Pope.

However, both Rome and the archdiocese remained silent until September 2, 1949, when the *Pilot,* the archdiocese's weekly paper, published an official censure by the Vatican of Father Feeney and the St. Benedict Center. An unofficial English translation gave a detailed account of the doctrine of salvation, upholding Archbishop Cushing and the Jesuits of Boston College. The censure ended with the injunction that after Rome has spoken, those churchmen who go against the Church cannot be excused even by reasons of good faith.

The *Pilot* added a footnote asserting that Father Feeney had declined an invitation to come to the Archbishop's residence and hear the decision ahead of publication. Nor, it said, would Father Feeney then listen to a reading of the contents at his center by a deputation from archdiocesan headquarters.

However, Archbishop Cushing, commenting on the situation, said:

"As the shepherd of the Archdiocese of Boston, my heart goes out in love to Father Feeney and to those who have been misled by false ideas. It is my fervent hope that now, after the supreme authority of the Church has spoken, Fathe Feeney and all his followers will prove themselves all to be loyal children of the Church and of our Holy Father, Pope Pius XII."

But Father Feeney's reply was, "Why don't they release the whole letter? It is possible that the letter may have criticized them, themselves."

Nevertheless, Father Feeney visited the Archbishop a few days afterward. What transpired has been told only in Father Feeney's words. He said he kissed the Archbishop's ring and greeted him as "my father."

Father Feeney recounted that he added, "I'm glad to see that I'm still your son."

Later, in a memorandum of the controversy published by the center, Father Feeney quoted Archbishop Cushing as saying he could only take his doctrine as it came to him in the letter from Rome. Father Feeney did not quote the prelate directly.

But, according to the center's account of the confrontation, Father Feeney finally arose and said, "In the name of the Blessed Virgin Mary, I accuse you of heresy." On that note, said the account, the meeting ended.

The St. Benedict group's memorandum asserted, "The issue is—why was Father Feeney suppressed by Church authorities for holding and professing that there was no salvation outside the Church?"

73

Notwithstanding having received every penalty short of excommunication, Feeney and his followers continued to preach their own doctrine of salvation. It was based on the "Decree of the Jacobites, in the Bull, 'Cantate Domine' of the Council of Florence under Pope Eugenius IV in 1442." This read:

> The most Holy Roman Church family believes, and professes and preaches, that none of those existing outside the Catholic Church, not only pagans, but also Jews and heretics and schismatics, can have a share in life eternal; but that they will go into the eternal fire, 'which was prepared for the devils and his angels,' unless before death they are joined with Her; and that so important is the unity of this ecclesiastic body that only those remaining in this unity can profit by the sacraments of the Church unto salvation, and they alone can receive an eternal recompense for their fasts, their almsgiving, their other works of Christian piety, and the duties of a Christian soldier. No one, let his almsgiving be as great as it may, no one, even if he pour out his blood for the name of Christ, can be saved, unless he remain within the bosom and the unity of the Catholic Church.

Although it must have been obvious that this document had been superseded by more recently promulgated doctrine, Father Feeney and his followers continued to defy the Church and to assume increasingly fanatical postures. A news agency quoted "an unimpeachable Vatican source" as saying that Father Feeney and his flock faced possible excommunication if they did not repent. In October, 1949, Father Feeney received notice of his dismissal from the Jesuit order, signed by the Superior General in Rome. The following year, the St. Benedict Center lost its official approval from the state board of collegiate authority. Veterans who attended it would no longer receive financial aid under the G.I. Bill. The enrollment at the time was 74, of whom 14 were under the bill.

By that time Father Feeney and a hard core of followers had taken a vow to devote their lives exclusively to preaching their views on Catholic faith. They called themselves "The Slaves of the Immaculate Heart of Mary."

The men donned black suits and ties, similar to the garb of fledgling seminarians. The women also donned black similar to but less enveloping than the garb of nuns.

Every Sunday afternoon for several years, in good weather and bad, the St. Benedict group held a preaching session on the south side of Boston Common. There, Father Feeney and others inveighed against Archbishop Cushing and the archdiocesan administration, against Jews and against Protestant Christians. And they yelled imprecations at bystanders whom they recognized, such as newspapermen or passing clerics of other denominations.

In addition, Father Feeney began writing a monthly four-page publication called *The Point,* in which he attacked Jews, Masons and Protestants indiscriminately. The original dispute was almost neglected.

Clad in their semireligious garb, the order began sending groups into cities along the Eastern Seaboard and as far west as South Bend, Indiana, and Chicago. They sold copies of books written by Father Feeney and other followers, expounding their views.

Members of the group were arrested in several communities and forcibly ejected from various places by police. Occasionally they were put under protective custody by the police.

One of the most ambitious forays was undertaken September 26, 1952, when 25 young men from the center invaded the residence of the Most Rev. Amleto Giovanni Cicognani, Apostolic Delegate to the United States, on "Embassy Row," in Washington, D.C.

When they were told that the archbishop did not receive such delegations, they virtually stormed his office, reporting later that Archbishop Cicognani, when asked if Father Feeney had been excommunicated, had replied no. The delegation left under heavy police surveillance.

Finally, on February 19, 1953, the *Pilot* announced that the Sacred Congregation had declared Father Feeney excommunicated for "stubborn disobedience to an order legitimately enjoined upon him to appear in Rome before the authorities of the Sacred Congregation."

Father Feeney not only declined to accept the announcement as official but he also stepped up his attacks on non-Catholics.

A source in Rome said that the Pope had made every effort to save the priest from excommunication. The source said, "We never saw him so anxious to help; he went out of his way to save him, but Feeney would not take advice."

In July of 1953, six of the Feeney group were escorted off the campus of the University of Notre Dame after creating a disturbance. One of the Cambridge travelers told a crowd, "The first sign of your approaching damnation is that Notre Dame has Protestants on its football team."

Two days later, on July 31, the same six were jailed in Chicago for disorderly conduct. They tried to force their way into the office of Samuel Cardinal Stritch. One of them said their purpose was "to ask him if Father Feeney is still a priest and will be forever. If so, it is his duty to correct the error of being called an ex-priest in the newspapers."

Nothing has so infuriated Father Feeney—outside of the main controversy—as to be called "Mr. Feeney" by news writers. He invoked the Biblical passage that "a priest is a priest forever after the order of Melchizedech."

A final public denunciation of the Feeney group was issued on September 6, 1955, by the three co-chairmen of the Boston chapter of the National Association of Christians and Jews condemning the actions of the Feeney group and stating: "It is disgraceful that such a group exists, and particularly that it should take such action in an effort to create hatred and misunderstanding among our people."

The occasion for the statement was the Feeney group's violent reaction to the erection on the Brandeis University campus in Waltham, Massachusetts, of three contiguous chapels—Protestant, Catholic and Jewish. Their particular target was the Jews, who had sponsored the university, in 1948, under nonsectarian principles. Their distribution of hate literature on Boston Common led to their being set upon by angered bystanders. The police finally gave the Feeneyites protection by loading them into patrol wagons and driving them several blocks away.

In 1957, the Slaves of the Immaculate Heart of Mary ran into difficulty with the city of Cambridge over building inspection codes. The group had acquired through purchase or rental a congerie of houses near the center. The question arose as to whether they were single homes or boardinghouses.

Eventually, the group sold its property and invested a reported $35,000 in a 20-acre tract of land, with a rambling colonial home, in the town of Harvard, about twenty miles west of Cambridge. They are still there.

Throughout the period when the controversy was raging at its hottest, the Archbishop refrained from adding to his formal statement, publicly. But he was known to have been deeply moved by compassion toward Father Feeney as a person; and in view of his own efforts toward achieving unity among all religious groups of Boston, the whole long episode must have been painful and embarrassing to him.

Fifteen years later, in a talk before the Massachusetts Clerical Association, an organization of Protestant Episcopal clergymen, at Trinity Church, on February 3, 1964, the prelate said that Christians should recognize the obstacles of differences in dogma, "but we must not quarrel over them." He went on:

"We are told there is no salvation outside the Church— nonsense!

"Nobody can tell me that Christ died on Calvary for any select group!"

Then, with a sly twinkle, he commented, "As the feller says, 'It is great to live with the saints in Heaven, but it's hell to live with them on earth!'"

CHAPTER VII

In Defense of Religious Freedom

SINCE Boston has long been a hotbed of religious antagonism, it has never surprised anyone that the more militant
Protestant ministers have carried on an unremitting campaign against the dangers of Catholicism. One such is the
Rev. Dr. Harold J. Ockenga, pastor of Park Street Church,
who has for the last twenty years been an exponent of the
Congregational faith founded on the fundamentals of
Biblical revelation, in the historic edifice situated at the
southeast corner of Boston Common. The location is known
as Brimstone Corner, partly from the fire-and-brimstone
sermons of Dr. Ockenga and his predecessors, and partly
from the legend that gunpowder was stored in the basement
during the War of 1812.

The Park Street congregation was founded in 1808, the
same year that the Roman Catholic Diocese of Boston was
established. The present Park Street edifice, with its Christopher Wren spire, has long been a landmark in downtown
Boston.

Dr. Ockenga's sporadic skirmishes with Roman theology
included a sermon in 1948 expressing his opinion that a

parade of members of the Catholic Youth Organization, made up of teen-agers, was reminiscent of the marches of children in Germany under Hitler and in Italy under Mussolini.

The *Pilot*, carrying a news story of the 80,000 youngsters who had paraded, also published an editorial answer to the Park Street minister. After describing the sight of the marching host, the *Pilot* went on:

> But as darkness crept along the city streets, its blackness found a strange home in one human heart, for music still echoed around the golden dome of the Capitol when a man rose up in one of Boston's most venerable pulpits and claimed to see in this display a threat to the future of the world. He was reminded by the bands and the marching feet of the sights he had seen in Italy and Germany and he wondered if what happened there was now appearing here. There are some it seems who don't know a child's step from a goose step, nor a parade from a rehearsal for war. Or perhaps there are some who, unable to trust their own motives, refuse to trust the motives of others.

Two years later, when Pope Pius XII proclaimed the doctrine of the Assumption of the Virgin Mary into Heaven as an intercessor for human sinners, Dr. Ockenga asserted in a sermon that undoubtedly the divine purpose of the proclamation was to prevent an overemphasis of "the human aspects of our Redeemer."

But he assured the Park Street congregation that "all that is necessary for salvation and morals is contained in the Bible." And to insure his message's being more widely received, it was published as a paid advertisement in Boston newspapers on November 8.

Dr. Ockenga declared:

"Let us give the Blessed Virgin Mary all the glory and

honor and esteem she deserves according to the Bible, but let us take care lest we do more and fall into the error of human cults which all had women prominent in their liturgy."

The following year, when President Truman, a warm friend of Archbishop Cushing, appointed General Mark Clark as United States Ambassador to the Vatican, Dr. Ockenga took umbrage.

He asserted that this was "the culmination of a long process of political aggression on the part of the Roman Catholic Church.

"This should be," Dr. Ockenga exclaimed, "the opening gun in the greatest battle for the American principle of separation of church and state this nation has ever seen."

But Catholicism continued its growth in the Boston community without bloodshed. And in 1952 the city government, preparing to turn Boston Common into a Christmas festival setting, announced that the Paulist Fathers would celebrate a public mass there at noon the day before Christmas. This would be followed at 4 P.M. by a service to be conducted by the Very Rev. Edwin J. van Etten, dean of the Episcopal Cathedral Church of St. Paul. Dr. Ockenga issued a public protest.

This, said the Park Street parson, was "a violation of our nonsectarian religious traditions." And he called on all citizens to protest vocally and by letter to the city fathers and to the newspapers.

Dr. Ockenga contended that while he was not opposed to religious services on the Common, he objected to sectarianism being introduced into a city celebration.

"I defend anyone's right to preach on the Common," he said, "but it should not be identified with a civic function."

He continued:

81

"We Bible Protestants believe mass is idolatrous in that the Roman Catholics teach that bread and wine become the blood of Christ through the blessing of the priest."

But Mayor John B. Hynes, a Catholic, declined to retreat. And in face of the possibility of embarrassment to lesser ranking clergy, Archbishop Cushing appeared in person to celebrate the mass.

"It would be strange, indeed," said the prelate from the altar, "if the holy sacrifice of the mass, which is so welcomed on the battlefields, were not welcomed within the peaceful precincts of the Common."

There the matter ended. The Roman Catholic mass not only went off without a hitch but Dean van Etten also had an unruffled service in the Anglican tradition in the afternoon.

The Rev. Dr. Ockenga's fulminations seemed minor indeed compared to the new prejudice against the Church that was given impetus by the suppression of Roman Catholicism in the Communist countries of Europe.

Archbishop Cushing's experience as director of the Boston office of the Society for the Propagation of the Faith, and his long association with missionaries from all parts of the world, had given him an early warning of the menace of Communism to all religious faiths, and he was acutely aware of the sufferings of fellow Catholics in Communist countries. If the marching of children's feet brought visions of Hitler and Mussolini to Dr. Ockenga, Cushing was even more perturbed by the fate of Catholic prelates in Yugoslavia and Hungary. In 1947 it gave him particular pain to have to defend the faith against a group of Protestant clergymen who, after a visit to Yugoslavia, had affirmed that Catholics, including the imprisoned Archbishop

Aloysius Stepinac, enjoyed freedom of worship. To find that Protestants, with whom the Church had established a modus vivendi, however precarious it seemed at times, were virtually giving their approval to the Church's sworn enemy caused the Archbishop to protest with all his conviction.

The seven Protestant clergymen were Dr. Guy Shipler, editor of the *Churchman*, an unofficial Episcopal magazine; the Rev. William H. Mellish, associate rector of Holy Trinity Church, Brooklyn; the Rev. Emory Bucke, editor of *Zion's Herald*; the Rev. George Buckner, editor of the *World Call* of the Disciples of Christ; Dr. Samuel Trexler, president of the Lutheran Synod of New York; Claude Williams, director of the People's Institute of Applied Religion, Birmingham, Alabama, and Philip Elliott of the First Presbyterian Church, Brooklyn.

In a ringing speech that drew the plaudits of fair-minded Christians of all faiths, Archbishop Cushing denounced the seven clerics for what he considered anti-Catholic positions. The occasion was an address before more than 1,000 Knights of Columbus at their 65th National Convention in Boston, in which the Archbishop asserted that "seven hand-picked American Protestant clergymen had signed an infamous monstrous document" when they testified that Roman Catholics and Archbishop Stepinac enjoyed freedom of worship in Yugoslavia.

"It is with pain and regret that I denounce these men and their campaign of misrepresentation and malice," said the prelate. "I denounce it nevertheless."

In a half-hour speech that was by far the most vigorous since his elevation, Archbishop Cushing expressed hope that "responsible Protestant leaders, who respect religion and who know what democracy is, will repudiate these unhappy instruments of irreligion, these apologists for an anti-democratic, anti-religious dictatorship.

"I think it is high time," said Richard Cushing with cold, measured tones, "that someone said what everyone knows: the wave of anti-Catholicism and particularly of foreign-inspired anti-clericalism, which is gaining momentum in the United States and elsewhere at the moment can no longer be dismissed as being due to 'crackpots' or irresponsible fanatics disavowed by their own non-Catholic churches or committees.

"Neither can it be dismissed as a superficial thing aimed only at certain Catholic practices, privileges or persons," he went on. "With pain as an American, with profound reluctance as a priest, I feel bound tonight publicly to denounce the systematic and sinister anti-Catholicism or organized groups like the committee of ministers which last week returned to this country from Yugoslavia to fulfill the promise they made to Tito and to themselves proclaimed in the press to sell to the American people the Red Fascist line with regard to what is happening to religion in Eastern Europe."

Calling on the Knights to join in denouncing the campaign, Archbishop Cushing warned that "if the Red agent-provocateurs succeed in enlisting the support of more professedly religious leaders like this committee, then it may happen here more speedily than you think."

Poison was being spread, the Archbishop asserted, "not by wily political agents, but by men who—may God forgive them—are introduced as 'reverend' and who ask to be heard as the representatives of Christ.

"I warn you," he declared, "we live in evil and dangerous times when things can happen like the sellout to

Tito of the seven Protestant clergymen who were hand-picked to defend before the American people, Tito's war on religion.

"If these times eventually come to their logical issue, you and I may live to see that day when like committees will visit American bishops in their prison cells and will release to the scandalized public smug assurance that all is well —that religious freedom is intact because the imprisoned bishops are allowed to pray in private and are given food to eat."

Aloysius Stepinac had been sentenced to sixteen years in prison by the Yugoslav government in 1946 for alleged collaboration with the Nazis in World War II. He was released in 1951, elevated to Cardinal in 1952 and died in 1960.

Cushing expressed reluctance to discuss the situation because he realized that "Communist strategy is to divide Christians one from the other.

"Then, too," he said, "I promised when I first became archbishop to desist from all argument with our non-Catholic neighbors and from all purely defensive talks about Catholicism.

"I certainly prefer to be a good neighbor. I still do. But actions like those of Tito's clerical committee are more provocative than I can bear, more than a priest should bear. And, in any case, I refuse to believe that these hand-picked friends of Tito represent the non-Catholic Christian community."

Commenting on the Archbishop's address, Dr. Bucke asserted that the Archbishop had been "misinformed." He said that the group had visited the head of a Catholic theological school in Zagreb, a Serbian Orthodox seminary in Belgrade and a Jewish rabbi in the course of compiling their report, which found no restriction of religion under the Tito regime.

Dr. Bucke commented that "it is to be expected that the Catholic hierarchy will not be pleased with the separation of church and state which Marshal Tito is bringing to pass."

In a subsequent editorial in *Zion's Herald,* Dr. Bucke wrote, "We saw to our own satisfaction that the right to worship according to the dictates of one's own conscience was in no way curbed by government policy."

Dr. Shipler concurred with that finding and asserted, "I am fully aware that the facts in the case of Archbishop Stepinac, the quisling collaborator with Hitler, for example, are the last things the Roman hierarchy wants reported in this country or elsewhere.

"If the Roman Catholic church in America wishes to be free from criticism," said Dr. Shipler, "let it become only a church and not a political state.

"Every decent Protestant respects the constitutional rights of Roman Catholics, but increasing numbers are determined to fight the type of political clericalism which has been so disastrous to other countries."

The Boston *Herald,* which has a wide Protestant readership, staunchly supported Archbishop Cushing's stand. It asserted, "We believe that Archbishop Cushing was on sound religious ground, and spoke for American principles in such things, when he attacked the report of the clergymen and the circumstances of their visit.

"His anxieties bring us back to our own previously expressed concern for that segment of the Protestant clergy which seems all too willing to be taken in by Soviet semantics," said the *Herald.* "They are the Henry Wallaces of the Protestant Church."

Archbishop Cushing did not relent in his attack on Communism as a threat to civilization.

In a speech in February, 1949, discussing the imprisonment by the Communists of Joseph Cardinal Mindszenty in Hungary, Archbishop Cushing declared, "It is an easy thing to imprison a cardinal or an archbishop or even suppress priests, but it is impossible to stifle hundreds of millions of the faithful in all the countries of the world."

One of his strongest speeches on the subject was made on June 15, 1950, in Cleveland, to the mid-century convention of the Newman Clubs of colleges in the United States.

"Communism," said Archbishop Cushing, "displays a set of generic ideas that are false but ideas in which it passionately believes and for which it is willing to die.

"There appears to be no comparable passion for our ideas among us in the West. The talk about democracy, freedom, representative government, is woefully inadequate. It is mostly talk and very little more. It deals for the most part with pure form, the external machinery of government, housing, job seeking and community relations of the most superficial kind.

"But it is not on the sublime level of ideas which inflame. It does not satisfy man's deepest cravings for friendship and understanding, for truth and love.

"It has lost its Christian heart. It has lost its Catholic soul. It has lost its 'guts'!"

A pamphlet written by the Archbishop, containing a series of questions and answers about Communism, has been reprinted in more than a dozen languages. It is a sort of catechism of anti-Communism.

From his remarks to the Newman Clubs it was evident that the Archbishop was concerned not merely with direct attacks on the Catholic Church by Communists but by a secular spirit in the life of a democracy which tended to regard all religion as politically suspect, and to impugn the patriotism of American Catholics. Shortly after his attack on the seven Protestant clergymen in 1947, Archbishop Cushing spoke again on the subject. He told more than 5,000 delegates to a national convention of the Holy Name Society in Boston that a new bigotry was sweeping the country. He said this was a doctrine that "there is a fundamental antagonism between Catholicism and Americanism.

"I speak for perhaps 25,000,000 Catholics who live their lives completely confident of the perfect harmony between their duties as Catholics and their duties as Americans," said the Archbishop in ringing tones that rose above a tumult in the audience.

"No need of my naming them, these two leaders of the new bigotry," he asserted, "but we do not intend, as Catholics, to abdicate our rights, or those of our little children, simply because one bigot says that we should."

Most of the delegates immediately concluded that the two persons the Archbishop had in mind were Dr. Shipler and Bishop G. Bromley Oxnam of the Methodist Church in New York. And the assumption was never refuted.

Archbishop Cushing said that the old-fashioned bigotry against the Catholic Church was dead, but that a new kind had arisen.

"It is being said with increasing frequency," said the prelate, "that while Catholics are undoubtedly loyal enough to their faith they do not mean what other Americans mean when they talk of freedom and that their religious principles concerning freedom make them a menace to the freedom of others in any community where they become a power."

Archbishop Cushing recalled the religious clash that marked the 1928 Presidential campaign when Alfred E. Smith was the Democratic nominee. The prelate said that Smith's post-election prayer that "never again in this land will any public servant be challenged because of his faith" had never been answered. And he commented that there were disturbing signs that it would not be for years to come.

"For example," said Archbishop Cushing, "the editor of an anti-Catholic religious magazine and one of the largest publications of his denomination, has called for a non-Catholic bloc to protect American institutions from the danger of Catholics in places of trust.

"Again, a leader in another denomination, perhaps the largest religious group in America, constantly returns in his public addresses to the theme of the alleged lack of sympathy between Catholic thought and democratic thought.

"This particular critic of Catholics frequently adopts the argument that non-Catholic religions are concerned with the development of civil liberty, while Catholicism inevitably leads to despotism and intolerance. He even declares that democratic systems are forms of government natural to non-Catholics and implies that Catholicism finds tyranny more congenial to its ideas. Wherefore, he warns those who love liberty to beware and to bedevil the organized Catholic Church."

However, the Boston prelate commended to his audience the sentiments of the Rev. Douglas Horton, a Congregational church leader. Again without mentioning any name, Archbishop Cushing said that "another non-Catholic leader has recently circularized his brothers in the ministry, asking them to be on their guard against becoming participants of the renewed anti-Catholicism which this good neighbor fears is sweeping America.

"I share that fear," he went on. "I do so principally as an American. In the long run, only America stands to suffer from artificially fostered bigotry of the type promoted by these men."

The Archbishop said that the differentiation between Catholicism and Americanism did not represent the true sentiments of non-Catholics in general, but he asserted that "it is annoying constantly to have to produce our credentials and to prove that we are entitled to the common political rights of other human beings in our own land."

In December, 1947, Archbishop Cushing disclosed to an audience at a Knights of Columbus anniversary banquet in Concord, Massachusetts, that he had been deluged with critical and sometimes abusive letters for his defense of Catholicism. But he called for charity.

"By example, we must show them we are not enemies, but true and sincere friends," said the prelate. "If we are to muffle the attack of those who would attempt to destroy the Church, we must be armed with the only worthwhile defense, a true knowledge of the Church, its dogmas and its history. We must, every member of the Church, be a personal representative of the Catholic Church and live an exemplary life dedicated to the ideals of our faith and the sacrifice of Christ."

Again in the 1950's the issue of Catholic patriotism and political power was raised by the publication of a book, *American Freedom and Catholic Power,* by Paul A. Blanshard, a self-appointed critic of Roman Catholicism. His general thesis, that Rome and Moscow had something in common in the struggle for men's minds, struck a responsive chord among Protestants and for several years he worked up an active speaking schedule under the sponsorship of such groups as Protestants and Other Americans United for Separation of Church and State. During his moment in the spotlight, he made one or two visits to the Boston area. Mr. Blanshard said, "No one questions the patriotism of the Catholic people as loyal Americans, but we have a right to criticize the policies of their leaders when these policies conflict with American traditions."

The Roman Catholic Church, said Mr. Blanshard, "has a perfect right to maintain a separate and competing school system, but it should not ask for public funds for church enterprises in all countries where the church is strong." He also asserted that Catholic parents were "threatened with theological penalties if they send their children to public school against the wishes of their priests." Before he gradually dropped out of the spotlight, Mr. Blanshard, a former State Department aide, unsuccessfully tried to have the citizenship of Archbishop Gerald P. O'Hara, a native Pennsylvanian, revoked on the ground he was serving as the diplomat of a foreign power in accepting a papal order to go to Ireland as apostolic nuncio.

The Blanshard book was listed in Catholic newspapers and magazines as "totally objectionable for general reading." But that directive made it clear that it was not banned for students, who read it widely and discussed it in Catholic schools and colleges. The clergy severally found the book irritating or amusing. But the laity for the most part found it galling.

Finally, Archbishop Cushing for Bostonians summed it up by saying:

"What have the Catholics of this country ever done that their loyalty should be called in question by anyone? Have we ever taken up arms against our government? Have we ever plotted its overthrow? Is a century or more of good conduct no argument in favor of the Church in this country?

"With almost 30,000,000 Catholics, we exercise less influence on the thought of this country today than some of the weakest Protestant sects, though we number almost half of the active membership of all churches combined. Catholic religious power is therefore great, but it is false and vicious to talk of Catholic 'political' power."

CHAPTER VIII

Secularism vs. Religion

DESPITE the Archbishop's denial of the existence of Catholic political power, intimations of it inevitably keep cropping up in controversies involving the Catholic faith. And adversaries of the faith are quick to seize upon any Catholic position which appears to have a political aspect.

Richard Cushing has been compelled to joust with every kind of non-Catholic opponent. His controversies with the Jewish community have been marked by somewhat less acrimony than has characterized his frays with the fire-and-brimstone Protestants, or with Communist sympathizers. He has always had cordial relations with Boston's Jews. One of his sisters is the widow of a Jew to whom she was happily married for thirty-four years. A leading Jewish layman, Sidney Rabb, who has been involved in some of Cushing's charitable activities, has commented that to him the Cardinal "has all of the attributes that a man in the image of God on earth should have."

Nevertheless there have been passages at arms with Jewish leaders when Cushing has had to assert Catholic principles on specific issues.

For several years during the 1950s, an adoption case that involved the child of an unmarried Catholic nurse and a Jewish couple who took custody of it became a favorite feature of the tabloid press, especially the Hearst newspapers. The incident became known as the Hildy Ellis case.

The nurse, twenty-one-year-old Marjorie McCoy, was found during a routine physical examination to be pregnant. The unnamed father was reported to be an intern and a Protestant. The girl's mother, anxious to keep the matter as quiet as possible, arranged through a physician friend to have the child adopted soon after it was born.

Although Marjorie was suspended when her condition became known, she was admitted to the hospital to be delivered of her baby, a girl, on February 23, 1951. Eleven days later, on the steps of the hospital, the child, Hildy, was handed over to Mr. and Mrs. Melvin B. Ellis of Brookline, for $500 and hospital fees totaling $157. The Ellises operated a dry cleaning establishment. Each had been married before and divorced. There were no other children.

A couple of weeks after the Ellises took the child, they filed a formal petition of adoption in Norfolk County probate court, only to discover that Marjorie's signature on the petition had not been properly notarized. When the girl visited the office of the Ellises' lawyer to correct the error, she was told that her baby had been placed in a non-Roman Catholic home. She was not told then that the Ellises were Jewish. But she was assured that the petition would not be allowed for at least a year, so that she would have plenty of time to think things over and change her mind, if she chose.

Marjorie McCoy immediately began to have misgivings. And when she read a copy of the state adoption laws, left with her by a social worker from the State Division of

Child Guardianship, the girl decided to see about having Hildy placed with the Catholic Charitable Bureau until a Catholic home could be found. The crux of the matter was an amended section of the law, adopted by the state legislature in 1950, asserting that probate judges "when practicable, must give custody to persons of the same religion as that of the child."

But the Ellises, having become attached to the child and believing they had acted in good faith, refused pleas to surrender Hildy. This touched off a series of court actions extending over the next six years. The Ellises finally left the state, only to be arrested in Miami by a Massachusetts state trooper in March, 1957. But Governor LeRoy Collins of Florida turned down a petition of extradition to Massachusetts for trial. The Ellises have since dropped out of the news, although they reportedly have returned to Massachusetts with the youngster, since renamed Judy. But in view of the changes in the religious climate, the case has faded from public memory, except among those closely associated with it.

While the case was being tried in the courts and in the newspapers, it underlined some of the sensitiveness of pluralism in Boston. To some of the Boston papers, the human interest aspects made the story a natural. To offset these, the *Pilot* published a series of articles more or less defending the official Catholic position on adoption. The legislature that adopted the 1950 amendment was heavily Democratic, which in Massachusetts at the time, meant a strong Roman Catholic coloring. It was the sort of situation that gave critics like Paul Blanshard much of their ammunition. To have a Jewish couple fighting to keep the child of a Roman Catholic mother added to the flavor of human interest.

95

When a Catholic judge, Edward Morley, took issue with the official position, the *Pilot* fired back: "We take second place to none, not even with Judge Morley, in our preoccupation with the welfare of the child to be adopted. We will not, however, share his secularist view that religion is either a minor or a negligible factor in the life of a child or anyone."

On November 19, 1955, the *Pilot* took the daily press to task editorially. Monsignor Lally wrote:

> The Ellis case is back in the news, and despite court orders, Catholic Hildy McCoy is still being held captive by the Jewish couple who refuse to return her to her mother.
>
> In connection with the news handling of the Ellis case we feel it necessary to remind our readers that some of the local papers have, apparently, decided to exploit the cheap emotional angles, and weep through their various editions. They have already begun by reprinting the brazenly partisan visit of a New York sob sister to the Ellis hideout.
>
> We must reluctantly acknowledge the irresponsibility of those in the daily papers who have stooped to this mocking of justice. In fairness to its readers, the *Pilot* will be forced to make individual references to future violations.

In the legislature, an attempt to modify the adoption law to permit a mother to give her child for adoption to persons of another religion got under way. In view of the Hildy Ellis case controversy, it was doomed. But the *Pilot* took up the cudgels, to keep the record straight. It held that such a law would open up "opportunities for the revival of the black and gray markets with all the bargaining in babies which the legislature made impossible in the present law."

The *Pilot* also commented:

> The American Jewish Congress has shown a special in-

terest in this legislation and we are sympathetic with the difficulty Jewish families have in seeking children for adoption. This law, however, is not the answer to that problem. We would be more impressed with the Congress' claim of interest in the rights of young mothers if we had heard them speak out in the Ellis case. That Catholic mother is still trying to get her baby back from the Ellis family who are Jewish. The Congress, not a notably reticent organization, is yet to be heard in defense of the rights of the mother.

The *Pilot,* as the official organ of the archdiocese, had carried the Church's official comments on the case. Finally the Archbishop himself spoke out at a meeting of Catholic women. He did not mention the fact that he had had a Jewish brother-in-law, or that his relations with the Jewish community had been cordial. At this time he spoke only as a Roman prelate who saw the interests of his church threatened. Discoursing for more than an hour, Cushing described the subject as "delicate, perhaps even dangerous, but on which a word from me is long overdue." Perhaps he had in mind the frequent accusation that Catholics wielded political power.

Asserting that there had been "no neglect, delay and no equivocation on the part of the courts," Archbishop Cushing said that "there has been defiance and calculated delay on the part of those who took the child, and these have obviously been intended as means to spar for time to construct an atmosphere of such public confusion, emotional upset and general misinformation as may now be perceived in the public statements of selected clerical groups, in letters to editors, from people who clearly have no idea of the facts or the forces at work and the amazing attacks on Massachusetts and Hildy's mother which have been printed in the inevitable anti-Catholic magazines and a few national picture magazines.

"In spite of all the injustice suffered by a girl and her baby these last six years, one can be, as I think all of us are, sincerely sympathetic with the feelings and sentiments of those who took the baby," said the Archbishop. "After all, their case differs from that of people who might have taken money or an inanimate thing, in this essential respect; they took a child whom they or anyone else would speedily come to love and to whom they have become understandably and deeply attached."

But as for those "who have played on the sympathies and emotions of others in order to create an atmosphere indifferent to the conscientious rights of the baby's mother and to the majesty of the law, we can only cry, shame, shame, shame—and this particularly to those who pretend not to see the shame," Archbishop Cushing declared.

"I have read that Hildy's mother has been 'pressured' by that omnipresent pressure force, 'the Roman Catholic Church,' in making her valiant stand," the Archbishop went on. "I welcome this chance to give the lie to that familiar line of attack.

"The influence of the Church in this case has at no time been that of a pressure group attempting to influence the courts or even to act as an organized ally of the baby's mother," he said.

"The Church has had a lifelong influence, of course, on her legitimate outlook and action."

Marjorie McCoy had made, the prelate said, "at a terrible price to herself and her own peace of mind, a powerful contribution to exposing and ending the type of private placements which, however well-intended in individual cases, actually foster the unfortunate conditions by which the worst situations of the 'black market' in babies can only flourish.

"In years to come she will be saluted as one of those who chiefly contributed to the ending of that disgrace. She has alerted girls who may find themselves in trouble to the dangers, far beyond the worst other fears that may assail them, which may threaten their security and that of their babies if they do not turn immediately to established, trustworthy agencies prepared to protect them against individual doctors, lawyers or others not sharing the regard for conscience and for the common good which fortunately characterize the overwhelming majority of Massachusetts professional men, social workers and jurists."

In an epilogue, Monsignor Lally, who carried most of the Catholic burden until the Archbishop spoke, wrote his reflections of the case in the June 8, 1957, issue of *America*, the Jesuit weekly. It was reprinted by the Jewish Community Council of Boston for distribution to council representatives, as an information bulletin. It drew particular attention to the next to the last paragraph:

Finally, a word must be spoken about the heavy cloud of silence which enveloped the official Jewish spokesmen from whom we might have expected some kind of appraisal. It is easy to understand their embarrassment in the face of the manipulations of those who set out to make the Ellis case hinge on the religious issue. The clear Jewish record in the famed Finaly and Beekman cases would, however, have led us to believe that such spokesmen might have properly been counted upon here to stand on the side of the law and the rights of a mother. A people with a keen sense of justice, and not notably reticent in the past in bringing their cause to public notice, their silence in this

99

issue is woefully eloquent. Catholics would have felt a brother's embrace if what was readily admitted in private had been willingly made public."

If Jewish spokesmen did not speak for the public record of the Ellis case, they sprang to the ramparts five years later in the aftermath of the Supreme Court decision outlawing the New York Regents' prayer from public schools in that state.

The high court, on June 25, 1962, held that the reading of the official state prayer violated the Constitution. It led the way to another decision, June 17, 1963, contending that no state or locality might require the recitation of the Lord's Prayer or Bible reading as an opening exercise in public schools.

In its September 1 issue, *America* warned "our Jewish friends" editorially that a concerted drive on their part to eliminate all religious practices in the public schools might lead to an outbreak of anti-Semitism nationally.

America scored the decision as a step toward secularization of the country. The editors commented that there had been "disturbing hints of heightened anti-Semitic feeling" since the Supreme Court's decision.

This had come about, the editors indicated, because Jews were among those petitioning the court to bar the prayer and because Jewish groups had since been trying to promote a "climate of opinion" that would make it easy for the court to continue to make decisions supporting the "absolutist" view of separation of church and state.

Such "doctrinaire views," the editorial said, were being promoted, despite a diversity of opinion and policy among Jewish groups, by the American Jewish Congress and its counsel, Dr. Leo Pfeffer, and by two Reformed Jewish organizations, the Union of American Hebrew Congregations and the Central Conference of American Rabbis.

"These Jewish Agencies," the editorial went on, "make no secret of their view that a favorable climate of opinion will help stop legislation providing grants or loans to church-related institutions of higher learning. Such a climate is also seen as favoring the passage of bills that would provide Federal aid to public but not to parochial schools."

Predicting that such activity could lead to the banning of the Lord's Prayer and Bible reading, as it did of course, the editorial commented:

> We wonder, therefore, whether it is not time for provident leaders of American Judaism to ask their more militant colleagues whether what is gained through the courts by such victories is worth the breakdown of community relations which will inevitably follow them. What will have been accomplished if our Jewish friends win all the legal immunities they seek, but thereby paint themselves into a corner of cultural and social alienation?
>
> The time has come for these fellow citizens of ours to decide among themselves precisely what they conceive to be the final objective of the Jewish community in the United States; in a word, what bargain they are willing to strike as one of the minorities in a pluralistic society. When court victories produce only a harvest of fear and distrust, will it all have been worthwhile?

The *Pilot,* in its edition bearing the same publication date, supported the Jesuit magazine's point of view and asserted that "some of the promoters of secularism mentioned by *America* have replied with the charge that the editorial is a 'disservice to religious pluralism.' Nothing could be more mistaken. The *America* piece is the good advice of a friendly neighbor and deserves the thoughtful consideration of that portion of the Jewish community that has been too long silent on these questions. A false image is being foisted on the American people, one that can create mischief and incite ill-will; the true picture should replace it promptly. Truth will prove to be the friend of true pluralism and working democracy."

In Boston, the *Jewish Advocate* lifted its editorial voice to say, "The *Pilot* and *America* harp on one sour note: that Jews who fight against religious intrusions in the public schools are ganged up with secularists and atheists bent on removing 'Anything savoring of religion from the public schools.' This, of course, is an absurdity furthest from the truth. For the battle is to preserve religious neutrality and like all our cherished liberties must be constantly waged in defense."

The *Advocate* went on to ask the two Catholic organs, "Since when has a group lost the right to its opinion in this country and by what right does anyone, especially editorialists for a church group, issue veiled threats against fellow Americans of another faith with an upsurge of antagonism to it for possessing different views?"

Richard Cardinal Cushing, who had expressed his personal views in the *Pilot* that the court decision was "ridiculous," stayed out of the duel between the editorial writers. He found that "it is difficult to imagine how civic morality of an enduring kind can be taught on any other basis than that of religion."

Before the controversy died a more or less natural death, Rabbi Roland B. Gittelsohn, president of the Jewish Community Council of Greater Boston, wrote a letter to the *Pi-*

102

lot. Portions of it were published in the *Pilot* and all of it in the *Advocate*.

Rabbi Gittelsohn noted that "when Catholics of Boston stood behind their youngsters who were expelled from the Elliot public school some years ago for refusing to participate in religious exercises, they served their church well, they served God well, and they served America well."

He also recalled the *Pilot* had recorded, when Catholics fought to keep religious services out of the public schools, that " 'they [the Catholics] managed, in fact, to secularize the schools and to remove religion from education. Surely this was against their own basic principles, but the social situation forced them into it.'

"We follow then, a great tradition," wrote Rabbi Gittelsohn. "When you advise us that anti-Semitism and unpopularity will be the inevitable outcome, you forget, it seems to us, that you were able to survive such an ordeal, and able to provide a classic example of abiding faith in the American principles of religious freedom."

It seems apparent, from Richard Cushing's conflicts with non-Catholics, that his chief concern with the status of religion in a society where church and state are specifically separated by law is with a secularism that denies to religion any place in civic life. On one occasion he defended the right of the Church to maintain parochial schools "to promote the common good and to seek the salvation of our children through our own schools whenever and wherever these be needed."

The remarks were in answer to a declaration a week before by Dr. James B. Conant, then president of Harvard, that the dual system of education in the United States was divisive and harmful to the country.

"Dr. Conant's words," said Archbishop Cushing, "will bring great comfort and increased boldness in pressing the campaign of secularism against independent schools, above all, religious schools.

"To the rest of us, his words should be a warning of the direction of the battle and of the accelerated speed with which it is being waged."

Some years later, during national debate on Federal aid to education, the prelate asserted that it was wrong to oppose it "if you think the Catholic Church might gain an advantage and you dislike the Catholic Church." But, on the other hand, a Catholic demanding aid on the grounds that it would ease his tax burden would be equally wrong, he said.

An undistinguished, little-known, and almost forgotten address which Cushing as auxiliary bishop made on July 4, 1939, in South Boston gives a clue to the concerns that underlay his more portentous statements on issues of national and international significance. Naturally in a Fourth of July address a reference to the Declaration of Independence is obligatory. What this statement reveals is considerably more than perfunctory patriotism. Richard Cushing had never forgotten that he sprang from an underprivileged and at one time despised minority, whose only solace was the Church, and whose solidarity came from religion. The virtues of patriotism and religion are inseparable, he pointed out.

"It is only natural that there should be this dual service to God and country," said Bishop Cushing, "for the political ideals of our great country—that all men are created equal—spring from the religious ideal that all men are the children of God. The rights of man are not a gift from any godless revolution. They were not even a discovery of our signers of the Declaration of Independence.

"This noble declaration merely expressed the doctrine which the Church has taught since Christ, her founder, who first preached and died on the Cross to redeem mankind. All mankind. Not just the rich and powerful. Not this race or that. Not only kings and nobles. He redeemed all men, white and black, brown and yellow. Only man because of his immortal soul has rights. That is where the rights of man came from. They did not come from any political document.

"From the prejudices directed against the Catholics of early days we must learn tolerance, from the animosity shown the Irish in those early days we must learn respect for men of every race and every nation. From the rights denied to our predecessors in those early days we must learn to be constantly on our guard so that hereafter none of those rights shall ever be taken from us."

Taken together with his later observation that the only possible basis for an enduring civic morality is religion, these remarks illuminate the positions which Cushing as bishop and archbishop has assumed whenever the integrity of the faith, the patriotism of Catholics, and their rights as citizens have been threatened. They also indicate that the ecumenical spirit which has distinguished him as cardinal was not a result of his new eminence in the Church but a basic part of his character.

CHAPTER IX

One Hundred and Fifty Years

THE year 1958 marked the 150th anniversary of the founding of the Archdiocese of Boston, and the fourteenth year
year of Cushing's archepiscopate.

Richard Cushing could look back on fourteen fruitful
years as head of the Boston See. And, for all the smiles that
greeted his unofficial slogan, "We will take up a collection,"
the tall, lean prelate had met the challenge of one of the
fastest-growing archdioceses in the world. Physically, the
archdiocese covers about 2,500 square miles, from Salisbury
to the northeast, Plymouth and Rochester to the southeast
and inland, in a crescent, from Ashby to Hopkinton to
Plainville. Five of the commonwealth's fourteen counties
are included—Essex, Middlesex, Suffolk, Norfolk and
Plymouth. Numerically, in 1958, the million and a half
Catholics made up nearly half of the total population and
three-quarters of the 800,000 persons living in Boston.

Adding new parishes to the archdiocese, raising funds for
new schools and hospitals, speaking frequently at innumerable diocesan functions—all this kept him busy enough. In
addition immediately after the war he began to organize

and conduct pilgrimages of his flock to various shrines in the New World and the Old. A new generation was demonstrating amazing mobility and Cushing had the wit to take advantage of it. The port of Boston, once a major embarkation point during the war, saw a new flurry of activity as pilgrims sailed for overseas ports. Although he entered into this new activity with his customary gusto, it was plainly wearing and sometimes exasperating. On one occasion he had to dispatch an aide to a wire agency office in Rome to plead that a casual remark to a reporter should not go out over the international cables. He had said, "Don't ever go on a pilgrimage with a bunch of old women!" The remark was not sent out.

The appetites of the Boston Catholics having been whetted by an overland pilgrimage to the Shrine of Ste. Anne de Beaupré, outside of Quebec, in 1946, more than 400 signed up for a Holy Year pilgrimage to Rome, a year later. They visited St. Peter's to lend support to the beatification of Pope Pius X. The trip proved so successful that it was inevitable that 1949 would mark a pilgrimage to Ireland. When the Bostonians returned from that trip, they were accompanied by a community of Trappistine nuns of the Cistercian Order of the Strict Observance, whose professed members have a vow of silence. They marked the 24th religious community invited to settle in the archdiocese following the end of World War II. And they were followed by more than 40 others in the next dozen years.

By 1958, the 150th anniversary year of the diocese and a few months before he became Cardinal, Richard Cushing had seven pilgrimages behind him and was planning an eighth. The boy from the cold-water flats had become a world traveler. One of his accepted chores was to send chatty cables back to Boston for the daily newspapers as well as the weekly *Pilot*. Commenting on a fire drill on one voyage, Cardinal Cushing wrote, "If my opinion was asked, I would say that the women seemed to look better in life preservers than they did in their so-called sacks."

The transplanted Celt, of course, was in his element when one pilgrimage reached Dublin. He said at one state dinner, "I have come to Ireland on a special mission, a mission to pay a brief tribute to the tremendous contribution that Irish emigrants have made to the Archdiocese of Boston, which is now the second largest in the United States." He added with a twinkle, "We are more Irish in Boston than you are in Dublin." Before returning home, the Cardinal visited the little village of Glenworth, his father's birthplace, where he found a banner stretched across the street, reading, WELCOME HOME. In the village, Cardinal Cushing blessed a new school that had been named in honor of his father, Patrick. The Archbishop met one old tad, who said he could remember when Patrick Cushing said farewell to earlier villagers setting out for America.

One of the most momentous of his pilgrimages was taking 63 physically and mentally handicapped children to the Shrine of Our Lady of Lourdes, in France, in 1954. For all of his enjoyment of travel with active adults, the children's pilgrimage affected him visibly.

The departure from Boston attracted a throng of nearly 10,000. Most of them went to the observation deck of the airport terminal building at the request of the Archbishop, to avoid, he said, upsetting the youngsters. The sight was more upsetting to the elders.

The ailments of the children ranged through poliomyelitis to brain damage to cerebral palsy. More than half of them had to be carried aboard from two buses that brought them from the city. Many of the onlookers wept unashamedly as the prelate welcomed each child off the bus. Some of them were looking bewildered and even frightened, but invariably brightened at the sight of the Archbishop.

"If God in his wisdom sees fit to cure any one child, we shall, of course, be grateful," said the Archbishop, "but our trip will be made primarily to pay honor to Our Lady of Lourdes."

During the flight, Archbishop Cushing helped the nuns feed the children and keep them calm. There was a 30-minute refueling stop at Gander, Newfoundland, and when the prelate found that several children were feeling ill, he had them all taken off for a rest.

A gathering of church and state dignitaries, including President Sean T. O'Kelly of Ireland, was on hand at the Dublin airport. But despite the welcoming ceremonies, the Archbishop insisted on supervising the transfer of the children into buses that took them to Our Lady of Lourdes Hospital, in Drogheda, outside of Dublin, for the night. Also declining an invitation to stay at the home of President O'Kelly, the Archbishop said, "I am the leader of the pilgrimage and it is only right I should stay with my pilgrims."

But although he had had little sleep on the flight from Boston, Archbishop Cushing spent most of the following night roaming the corridors to make sure the children did not become frightened at the strange surroundings.

Again, on arriving at Lourdes-Ossun airport, the prelate turned down an invitation to stay with Bishop Pierre Marie Theas in favor of keeping watch over his flock at the nearby Mission de Marie Convent. The convent was at Barters, the village where fourteen-year-old Bernadette Soubirous tended her flocks a century earlier and told of seeing a visitation by a "beautiful lady in white." The waters of the Lourdes Massabielle Grotto, where Bernadette had her vision, have been credited with miraculous cures.

The Boston group spent three days at Lourdes, bathing in the waters, picking flowers on a nearby mountainside and attending religious services. On the last full day, Archbishop Cushing led a religious procession of 300 pilgrims through the streets of Lourdes.

The takeoff for Boston was delayed for an hour because of the enthusiasm of a throng on hand to give the 63 children and their guardians a send-off. Some hours out over the Atlantic, the No. 4 engine began sputtering. The pilot radioed ahead to Gander that he was feathering the engine and asked permission to make an emergency landing. With fire trucks and emergency equipment lining the runway, the craft came in without a hitch. And most of the children slept through the whole performance, blissfully unaware of the situation.

Realizing that news of the incident would reach home ahead of them, Archbishop Cushing telephoned Monsignor Lally in Boston to reassure parents and others waiting that all was well.

A Trans World Airlines plane was diverted to Gander to pick up the stranded group. But there was room for only 43 of the pilgrims, so all except the mentally retarded were put aboard. The Archbishop remained behind with them until a Pan American Airways plane could be sent up from New York. The Archbishop finally arrived in Boston twelve hours behind schedule and he was one of the two last persons off the plane. He led a small, mentally retarded boy by the hand.

It was pouring rain, but the Archbishop was happy. He called it all "the most inspiring, the most successful of any pilgrimage that I have sponsored. Please God, we're going back again next year." And he did.

For a man to whom a vacation was something other people took regularly, Richard Cushing's fourteen years as archbishop ran together in a series of crises, developments and amusing incidents. Nevertheless, he could joke under apparently serious conditions, but he could be grim and forbidding if something did not please him. And although the image he created was that of benevolent pastor, who seemed bewildered by all of the honors showered on him, he also was so unpredictable that anyone crossing him at the wrong moment could not believe the tongue-lashing he received came from the same man who the day before might have thrown an arm across one's shoulders with a paternal squeeze.

It was inevitable that the schedule that Archbishop Cushing imposed on himself would prove a strain on his health; and despite his efforts to preserve his personal privacy, he has been unable to hide a series of illnesses that have plagued him periodically since 1952. His schedule of public appearances is so full that his health becomes suspect whenever he misses one, and this has been accentuated as he has become more and more widely known. For years he has suffered from chronic asthma. He sleeps in a simple iron bed, but many nights he has spent dozing in a chair to ease his breathing. In more recent years, he has developed emphysema, a thickening condition at the base of the lungs that makes breathing even more difficult. He has acknowledged having two oxygen tanks in his bedroom for use during the night particularly.

As archbishop in 1952, Richard Cushing was sent to St. Elizabeth's Hospital for a week to see if he could shake off a particularly heavy cold. Throughout the stay, the prelate fretted about getting back to work. Then, the following year, in the midst of a full program of speaking, severe back pains impelled him to call his physician, who personally drove him to the hospital. A cryptic bulletin the following day said that the Archbishop would remain in the hospital for "a period of rest and a routine checkup."

After routine tests, the chancery of the archdiocese made the announcement that Cushing would undergo surgery to correct a minor disorder. The ailment was not related to his chronic asthma, and it was hinted that Cushing's heavy schedule of public appearances was a contributing factor. On December 8 the Archbishop underwent an operation to relieve a gall bladder condition and it was expected that he would remain in the hospital two or three weeks for convalescence. Special prayers were offered for the Archbishop, the date being that of the Feast of the Immaculate Conception, a day of holy obligation for Catholics. Later that month Cushing underwent an operation to correct a longstanding ailment, a cyst on the kidney. Both Major John B. Hynes and Governor Christian A. Herter issued public appeals for prayers; and in his Christmas message the Archbishop himself said that he stood in special need of prayers at the holiday season.

The second operation took 90 minutes but was reported as successful. The Archbishop's recovery was normal, although he had lost 20 pounds. He returned to his residence January 5 and three days later issued a statement to thank the public for their prayers, remarking that it would be some time before he could resume his usual schedule. A photograph released with the statement showed the Archbishop in as good health as could be expected. But the robust look of his earlier days was gone. The gaunt, craggy features now so familiar to Americans were beginning to show.

By March, the prelate was beginning to push himself once more, as if to make up for lost time. But, on the 16th, the eve of St. Patrick's Day, he collapsed during a speech in the Elm Street Theater in Worcester, Massachusetts, at a celebration by the Friendly Sons of St. Patrick.

The Archbishop began his address by joking about his health. He said:

"I weighed 205 pounds a few months ago. Now, I weigh 160. You'd better take a good look at me now because I don't know how much there will be left of me in a while."

A few minutes later, still speaking, Cushing began to sway. Bishop Wright moved to his side, but Cushing waved him away. Then the Archbishop collapsed as Bishop Wright and the other clergy on the platform moved in to support him. Refusing an ambulance, the Archbishop was driven to St. Vincent's Hospital in his own car, but before midnight he was home in his residence in Boston.

The official word from the chancery office the next day was that the prelate had collapsed from fatigue as the result of an exhausting schedule. The newspapers noted that he had lacked his usual vigor in recent appearances.

Yet, despite the Worcester incident, and a visit in the morning from his physician, Archbishop Cushing announced that he would resume his regular routine at once.

Pale and wan, the Archbishop appeared at 9:50 A.M. the same day at Holy Cross Cathedral, in the South End, to celebrate the St. Patrick's Day mass. A house guest, Bishop Cornelius Lucey of Cork, preached the sermon as if nothing unusual had taken place.

The cathedral was filled to overflowing. The congregation had not expected to see their Archbishop and a murmur ran through the building as the prelate entered the sanctuary in his robes and began the mass.

The service not only went off as planned but the Archbishop also plunged back into his routine, with no discernible letup until after he was elevated to Cardinal five years later.

A rumor that the Archbishop had had cancer was not confirmed until 1964, when he appeared on a television interview with Arch Macdonald on WBZ-TV. In answer to a direct question Cushing said he had had the prostate gland removed, then ten days later had a kidney removed on which there was an eight-pound tumor.

"About eight years ago," the Cardinal said, "they gave me eight months to live. Somehow or other I survived. The Lord chooses the foolish to confound the wise."

In spite of a load of work that would have killed an ordinary man years ago, the Archbishop has said that he hopes "to live to be a hundred and that the Queen of Heaven takes me in tow fifteen minutes before the devil knows that I am dead."

Much of the Cardinal's exhausting activity has concerned fund raising, for which he has a fine intuition and uninhibited talent. The needs for which he raises funds are as varied and often as unlikely as the sources from which he obtains them. The cause might be the need of a convent for a new clothesline, with an electric potato peeler thrown in. Periodically groups of nuns have been taken out to Fenway Park to see the Red Sox, or to a seaside amusement park to ride the roller coasters. Or the issue may concern a million-dollar school or hospital. Whatever the occasion

Cushing seems to know how to take up a collection and provide what is required.

Once, during the 1950s, the Archbishop was at St. Anselm's College, in Manchester, New Hampshire, for the installation of a new abbot. At a three-hour luncheon following the ceremony, Archbishop Cushing was in one of his expansive moods. After fixing his eyes on a local businessman whom he knew to be well off, the prelate suggested that the good man no doubt would be glad to "pick up the tab" for the spread. He did.

Then he launched into a characteristic anecdote. He recalled receiving a telephone call at his residence from the mother superior of a community of Trappistine nuns in Wrentham, Massachusetts, about 40 miles south. The Trappistines are Cistercian Nuns of the Strict Observance, who are under a vow of silence, run a dairy farm and are completely cloistered.

"Your Eminence," said the mother superior, with a fine sense of not wasting words, "come down at once, we have had a tragedy."

It was lunchtime, the Archbishop had two architects with him to discuss plans for two new high schools, and there were a number of other early afternoon appointments.

"Can't you tell me on the phone what's the matter?" the Archbishop asked hopefully.

"I can't do that at all," was the crisp reply of one permitted to speak only to cover the barest necessities in an emergency, to an outsider.

The Archbishop told his audience that for a moment he wondered if perhaps there was a revolt afoot in the convent. Within half an hour, munching a hot dog and a Coke, the Archbishop was on his way.

A little nun answered the door and said, "So, it's yourself, is it, well, the reverend mother is having her nap, so you go into the parlor and wait for her, the quiet will do you good."

The Archbishop tried to explain that he had canceled a lot of important appointments in order to answer an emergency call and perhaps the nun had better let the mother superior know he had arrived.

"You can call her yourself if you wish," replied the nun, "but I have to live here after you've gone and I've not got a living soul in this country should I have to leave, and I would if I disturbed her."

For three-quarters of an hour the Archbishop twiddled his thumbs. Finally, the mother superior floated in and said, "So, you got here."

"Look, Mother," said the prelate, in no mood for amenities, "I came down here right after you called. Now what's the trouble?"

"All our cows have gone dry," responded the superior.

"What!" thundered the Archbishop. "You brought me all the way down here for that?"

Undaunted, the mother superior said, a little more patiently, "Now, your Eminence, you don't understand. If there is no milk, we can't sell it. Then we get no money to buy our food, the nuns will starve and you'll have to close up this place and we'll all have to go back to Ireland where you brought us from. And besides, you told us that if we ever needed anything to call you and you'd come right down."

Archbishop Cushing, explaining in an aside that he came from a "leaky roof tenement" and knew nothing of cows, told the mother superior to "go out and buy twenty cows and send me the bill." On the way back to Boston, the

Archbishop said he asked his chauffeur how much a cow was worth and the car nearly went off the road as the man at the wheel turned his head to stare, unable to believe his ears.

A week later, when a bill for $6,000 arrived, the Archbishop said he called the convent to see if they had bought gold-horned cows, or something.

"They're wonderful milkers that we got at a bargain of $300 apiece," said the mother superior. "God bless them and you, and if anything else comes up, we'll call you!"

Cushing has a healthy respect for nuns, and when they ask a favor they are seldom refused. But there are limits to his indulgence. Years later, when he was a cardinal, he was approached in Rome by a group of Swiss nuns who wanted to know if he would support the ordination of women to the priesthood.

"I told them, 'I have espoused many hopeless causes in my day, some of them known as Cushing's Follies, but I have never considered that one; why, if I were to go to confession to a woman, I might as well confess on television!' " said Cardinal Cushing.

There were few ways of raising funds that the Archbishop passed up. Parish newspaper and old license plate drives were soon a fixture under the Cushing administration. Stacks of old newspapers and license plates outside every third house in a given community were a sign that the local Catholic parish was in the wastepaper market, or selling scrap metal.

Often, the drives gave Protestants a chance to empty their cellars as well, and they would form their own piles or add on to a neighbor's. The Archbishop made it clear that money recognized no religion.

One of the Cardinal's most faithful fund raisers has

been Mrs. Lutza Smith, wife of Lou Smith, operator of Rockingham Park Race Track in Salem, New Hampshire. They are Jewish.

Annually, at a time when the horses are running elsewhere, the Smiths open the track for a party for handicapped children. And they mark the occasion with a generous donation to the Cushing charity fund. Over a period of years, the Smiths have given $500,000 toward the Joseph P. Kennedy, Jr. Memorial Hospital for handicapped children. And although the original building was erected through funds from the Kennedy Foundation, a new wing has been named in honor of Lou and Lutza Smith.

Mr. and Mrs. Stanley Blinstrub are another husband and wife team that has played a leading role in the Boston prelate's charitable activities. Blinstrub's Village is a small-convention-hall-sized nightclub that will book only acts that a priest taking his mother out for dinner could see and hear without blushing. But it has also had a long history as the setting for Cushing dinners for the aged, testimonials to worthy citizens whose popularity would guarantee a generous sale of tickets earmarked for charity and for numerous other good causes.

Stanley Blinstrub was the son of a Polish nobleman, who came to the United States in 1907. And although he had money in the bank, a high school graduation gift from his father, he salted it away and went to work. Then years later, he opened a small restaurant, got out of the business in 1923 to go into home remodeling, took over Blinstrub's again in 1933 and has been at it ever since.

In recognition of his donations to charity, he was one of thirty-eight men invested into the Equestrian Order of the Holy Sepulchre of Jerusalem in St. Patrick's Cathedral, in

New York, in 1958. His wife was one of thirty women invested in the same ceremony. His own city honored him in 1961 at a dinner at the Somerset Hotel. The sponsors were members of the Caritas Guild, the liquor industry fundraising organization. "Without Stanley," said the toastmaster, "there would be no Caritas Guild." For although purple prose was not permitted in Blinstrub's, the bar was well stocked.

As archbishop and later as cardinal, Richard Cushing has been so associated with Blinstrub's that it has come to be known as the Boston Vatican. One legend, probably with considerable basis of truth, is that the day after the prelate was notified of his elevation to cardinal, a friend of Patrick J. (Sonny) McDonough's asked him if he had heard the news.

"Sure, I knew it hours ago," replied Sonny, a Boston Irish politician, "I saw the white smoke coming from Blinstrub's."

At a time just after World War II, when the area around Lawrence, Massachusetts, was in the depths of a textile depression, Archbishop Cushing set a fund-raising goal of $600,000 for a needed hospital. People shook their heads. But the Archbishop raised $1,161,000. And the hospital, Bon Secours, is situated on a hill in Methuen, Massachusetts. About the same period, the Archbishop, by then referred to as the best real estate operator in New England, acquired a plot known as the Searles Estate in Methuen for the site of a seminary for the Basilian Salvatorian Order of monks.

Still exhibiting a talent for "taking up a collection," the Archbishop also raised another $1,000,000 toward the establishment of Merrimack College in North Andover to fulfill

119

a demand for more college facilities for the Greater Lawrence area. The Augustinian Fathers were placed in charge.

Such accomplishments added ecclesiastical honors to the honorary degrees that he said he was collecting "in bunches like bananas." He eventually was made an honorary Basilian monk, a member of the Augustinians, the Dominicans, a founder of the New England Province of the Jesuits and a member of the Third Order of Saint Francis of Assisi. The prelate has said he would like to be buried in the habit of a Franciscan.

As demands for his appearance grew, the Archbishop more and more became as important to the newspapers as the Governor or the Mayor of Boston. It was an accepted ground rule that he would "wait for the photographers." That became almost as well known a slogan as "Let's take up a collection."

Once, at a convention of 500 women when the time schedule had to be kept, photographers or not, the Archbishop finally stepped to the center of the platform and said:

"The Archbishop died and went to Heaven. St. Peter met him at the gate, Michael was there and all the archangels. St. Peter came forward with arms outstretched to welcome him and escort him through the pearly gates; and the Archbishop looked toward St. Peter and said, 'Hold everything! Let's wait for the photographers!'"

It might be Cushing's predilection for the camera that has led him to submit to television interviews when he has turned down pad and pencil reporters. It was on a television interview after he became a cardinal that he disclosed that he twice prepared to enter the Society of Jesus—the Jesuits—but each time backed off, although he could not be sure why. Then with a characteristic fillip he added, "Ever since that time the Jesuits are happy that I didn't join them because if I did they would have lost their best benefactor."

But it was probably not a fascination with the camera but simply a knowledge of the value of public communications that led to the founding of an archdiocesan television center in 1954, with Monsignor Walter L. Flaherty as director. Programs have been carried to the general public by local commercial stations. The eventual granting of a commercial license by the Federal Communications Commission was the first to a religious group primarily interested in religious and educational telecasting.

"The commercial license means, of course, that we can accept sponsorship of our programs," Monsignor Flaherty noted.

The original studios were assembled at 25 Granby Street, in the Back Bay district, the same brownstone mansion once used as the residence of the late Cardinal O'Connell, and where he received young Father Cushing frostily one morning and started him on his career as a missionary without leaving Boston.

The Archbishop inaugurated the studios with the celebration of a pontifical low mass on January 1, 1955. Masses have originated from the studio every Sunday morning since then. Monsignor Flaherty attends each service and describes the steps of the mass for the audience. It was made clear from the beginning that only the servers and formal studio guests of the celebrant could satisfy their obligations to attend mass. The television audience, as well as the cameramen and other technical staff members, are required to attend some other mass before or after the program.

On August 23, 1957, observing his sixty-second birthday,

the Archbishop officiated at the first nuptial mass ever televised. Cushing previously had insisted that marriages be solemnized in the church proper, rather than in the sacristy or in a chapel, in order to give them sacramental significance rather than treat them merely as a social occasion; and he also had directed that mixed marriages be held in the church to give them full religious dignity. But, changing his directive for the occasion, he gave permission for the marriage of Miss Rita Marie McLaughlin, a member of the telephone workers' Our Lady of the Way Guild, and John J. Gallagher, a Korean War veteran, to be held in the studios of WBZ-TV, as a feature of the station's *Our Believing World* interfaith religious series.

Eventually the archdiocese created its own television station. It went on the air in the fall of 1964 on Channel 38, an ultra-high frequency band. It is a million-watt facility with a telecasting beacon on top of the 52-story Prudential Tower, architectural symbol of the new Boston. Its initials are WIHS-TV—IHS being the monogram for the Greek word Jesus.

As a figure of national eminence and the spiritual leader of a large diocese, Archbishop Cushing inevitably has had political influence, however much he might deny that there is such a thing as Catholic political power. He helped to defeat such social legislation as a proposed state lottery and a referendum to permit the dissemination of birth-control information. But it is a standing joke in Boston that he can do nothing about the Elevated tracks that run past the cathedral. As far back as 1949, a proposal was made to remove the structure and it was understood in the State House that the Archbishop was in favor of the move. But the tracks are still there and every five or six minutes a train thunders past the cathedral, although they have been known to slow down on such occasions as the funeral of a cardinal. Cushing has sometimes grumbled about it. When the Boston Braves departed for Milwaukee, Lou Perini, the owner, a contractor and a generous donor to Cushing's charities, was publicly criticized for moving the team. But the Archbishop suggested that it might be "a blessing in disguise."

"Perini's move might inspire those with civic pride in this city not to take too much for granted," he told a communion breakfast audience. "The move to Milwaukee could arouse the citizens of this community to undertake several courageous projects." He listed among them the razing of "that monstrosity of an elevated structure."

A few weeks later, following a confirmation service at his old parish, Sacred Heart, he made his customary walk down the aisle, asking questions. Singling out one boy, he asked, "Who made the world?"

"God made the world," replied the youngster.

Then, recognizing the boy as Michael (Corky) Cronin, he asked, "Who made the Red Sox?"

"Tom Yawkey," promptly replied the son of general manager Joe Cronin, right-hand man of owner Yawkey.

"You certainly know your Catechism," chuckled the Archbishop.

The last three months of the Boston See's 150th anniversary year were marked by three historic events. Pope Pius XII died on October 9. Fourteen days later, the jovial peasant, Angelo Roncalli, was elected successor to the Throne of Peter, taking the name of John XXIII. In November, Archbishop Cushing received the news that he had been elected to the Sacred College of Cardinals.

On December 8, with Cardinal Spellman of New York as a special guest of honor, the Cardinal-designate celebrated a solemn pontifical mass in the cathedral to mark the end of the 150th anniversary of the archdiocese.

In a tribute written for the 150th anniversary, Bishop Fulton Sheen, auxiliary to Cardinal Spellman and National Director of the Society for the Propagation of the Faith, said, "Archbishop Cushing is the priest's bishop because he has given to our generation a deepened sense of the spirit of poverty."

Although the Boston prelate had not taken a vow of poverty, he practiced it, said Bishop Sheen, asserting, "His soul is poor; that is why it has so much room for the riches of God's blessing.

"Though not all priests can live under Archbishop Cushing," Bishop Sheen continued, "he lives in the hearts of all priests; that is the only true greatness."

But to a million and a half members of his archdiocese, Cushing was a good deal more than a bishop's priest. The students in the parochial schools he had benefited, the patients in hospitals financed through his charities, the hundreds of children he had confirmed, the entire community that had felt the impact of his social welfare activities knew him as their own benefactor and leader; and the peasant who had risen to Pope and who was to bring about a renewal of the church and its place in contemporary life seemed to recognize in him an ally.

CHAPTER X

The Red Hat

AT 11 P.M., Sunday, November 16, 1958, the telephone rang in the archepiscopal residence. The Archbishop of Boston was still up, working on his weekly column for the next issue of the *Pilot*. A busy day lay ahead and he wanted to make use of the closing hours of the present day.

A little wearily, Richard Cushing picked up the receiver. The voice at the other end was Archbishop Cicognani, calling this time from Chicago. The call unofficially made him a member of the Sacred College of Cardinals by the grace of Pope John XXIII. As he recounted the moment, later, Richard Cushing said, "I was bewildered, so I thought I would call some of our very capable priests who are well trained in public relations and editing, but I found they were all asleep, so I went to bed; there was nothing else I could do."

In the morning, the new cardinal found it necessary to squeeze in a press conference. He commented, "While I was saying mass this morning for the nine sisters of the Archbishop's household—I'm a sort of mother superior to them—I heard the phone ring again and I sensed then that the news had become known.

"My first reaction was that the people around here prayed me into it," he told the reporters. "I'm happy because they're happy. There are those who become cardinals because of personal and extraordinary endowments and great personal contributions they have made to the Church.

"In my instance, I feel my selection is attributed to the one and a half million priests, religious and people of the Archdiocese of Boston."

He asserted that the appointment would not affect his activities and that "I shall continue to do what I always have been doing. I am mindful a priest is ordained not for himself but for others."

The press conference was briefly interrupted by a roar from outside. It was raised by 48 seminarians from nearby St. John's Seminary, who had just heard the news. The new cardinal walked outside and shouted jovially, "You can all have the day off!"

Soon afterward, the Cardinal—for he assumed the title as soon as his appointment was announced—set out for suburban Milton to preside at a funeral mass for a contractor whose firm had erected several buildings for the archdiocese.

From there, Cardinal Cushing went to attend a luncheon to the Peruvian ambassador to the United States at the Ritz-Carlton Hotel, in Boston. And at night, he celebrated mass in the Emmanuel College chapel, in the Fenway district, for the School of Theology for the Laity.

Before the end of another week, he had gone to Portland, Maine, to open a fund drive for a small new Catholic college, to Manchester, New Hampshire, for a similar drive for St. Anselm's College, had dedicated a Carmelite convent and attended two communion breakfasts the following Sunday.

As far back as 1948, a Washington columnist had predicted that the Boston archbishop would be given the red hat by Pope Pius XII. But a consistory came and went and there was no change in the Boston See.

Then, less than two months after Angelo Roncalli ascended the Throne of Peter as Pope John XXIII in 1958, he named Richard James Cushing of Boston among 23 new cardinals to strengthen the Sacred College. Roncalli was the third of thirteen children of a peasant farmer and his wife, who lived in the little Italian hill village of Sotto Il Monte, in Bergamo County. He showed early evidence of being marked for the Church. But he never lost touch with his beginnings. This may have attracted his attention to the blacksmith's son from South Boston. As the years marched on, the earthy peasant grew in priestly wisdom and in physical girth, a rotund figure with craggy features set off by generous-sized ears and with an infectious smile that reflected an outgoing warmth.

Appointed in mid-career Patriarch of Venice, Cardinal Roncalli outlined his views in an address to his flock. It had the same tones that a Richard Cushing might have sounded in a similar situation. Roncalli said:

"I come from humility and was raised amid modest and blessed poverty. I would like to recommend myself to your benevolence as a man who wants to be simply and above all your brother; amiable, easy to contact, and understanding. Don't look to your patriarch as a politician or a diplomat; look for the priest or pastor of souls and the style of the pastor is to count his sheep one by one."

On October 28, 1958, when the genial prelate was

elected by his peers as Pope, he was already seventy-seven years old. Many, including Archbishop Cushing of Boston, looked on the choice as a caretaker role for the aging cleric between the death of Pius XII and some rising younger church father.

Almost immediately, as if aware that the time was running out, Pope John began instituting reforms. Not the least was the decision to increase the size of the College of Cardinals. His selection of Richard Cushing was enthusiastically received in Boston. But the Archbishop did his best to discourage public demonstration. He made it clear that he did not want any special reception on his return.

Instead of a testimonial, he told 1,500 members of the Nazareth Guild of Telephone Workers at a communion breakfast, he would prefer to "move around" the deaneries and the smallest parishes, to meet people who are inclined to gather at such an occasion.

"You know," he said, "some of these people have never seen a cardinal, or even the robes of a cardinal, and now it is time for me to tell them of my gratitude for all they have done to me."

On the day the new cardinal left for Rome on one of four airliners chartered to carry the Boston party, 10,000 persons were on hand at Logan International Airport in Boston to wish him godspeed. The temperature was 23 degrees above zero, and as he mounted the steps of his plane, Cardinal Cushing admonished the crowd, "Go right home, now before you catch cold!"

On his arrival in Rome, Cardinal Cushing presented Stefan Cardinal Wyszynski of Poland a check for $25,000 for the education of Polish seminarians. The money had been sent him by thousands of Catholics in his archdiocese on the news of his elevation. It included a sum of $3,600 donated by members of the Boston Police Department from the proceeds of their annual ball.

"My idea was to reach someone behind the Iron Curtain who could help the Church," he told accompanying reporters. "If I could, I would do the same for Cardinal Mindszenty in Hungary, or Cardinal Tien of China.

"Cardinal Wyszynski is a dedicated man, living in a country where the best contribution he can make is preaching and encouraging people to hold fast and live Christian lives.

"Christ is stronger and more powerful than Marx," the Cardinal continued, "and Christ will act, through justice, liberty and charity, to overthrow slave states.

"Strangely enough, there is a large number of vocations for the priesthood in Poland, very large. The problem is to train these young men for the priesthood."

The Bostonian made it clear that the money would be spent for the seminarians in Paris or Rome, rather than behind the Iron Curtain. Cardinal Wyszynski, released from prison in 1956 and permitted to resume direction of Poland's church, had been in Rome since Pope John's election.

The Right Rev. Ladislaus Sikoras of Salem, Massachusetts, and Monsignor Lally, the *Pilot* editor, served as interpreters as the two Princes of the Church talked for more than an hour.

The following morning, 200 Bostonians knelt in the ancient underground crypt of St. Peter, below St. Peter's Basilica, to worship with their new cardinal as he celebrated mass.

Then in tones familiar to them all, Cardinal Cushing said, "You'll find enough places to visit and keep you occupied for the next few days. And there's always shopping. I suggest you go see all of Rome. We have a few activities planned, including two or three free dinners, and you may want to come over to the North American College when I am officially notified of the honor of my elevation."

Then, with a few words about Rome's cold-breeding winters, he told the pilgrims, "God bless you all, and take care of yourselves.

Two days after his arrival in Rome, the Cardinal was informed of the unexpected death of his sister, Miss Elizabeth Cushing, sixty-seven years old, in South Boston. His two other sisters, Mrs. Mary Pierce and Mrs. Anne Francis, and his nephew, the Rev. William C. Francis, returned home for the funeral. The Cardinal's brother, John E. Cushing, stayed on.

Cardinal Cushing celebrated a private mass for the repose of his sister's soul at the chapel in the convent of the Franciscan Missionaries of Mary, the morning before his official notification of being elevated.

That afternoon, having canceled plans to attend a luncheon at the graduate house of the North American College, Cardinal Cushing went to the Ciampino airport to bid godspeed to his two sisters and nephew as they flew home for the sister's funeral back in South Boston.

"Let God's will be done," said the prelate as he left the airport. "I'm no different from anyone else."

That night, he slept at the North American College. He was joined in the morning by Cardinal Cicognani, his old friend and the Apostolic Delegate to the United States, and John Cardinal O'Hara of Philadelphia. All three then gathered in a room off the ultra-modern dining hall of the college to await news from a secret consistory on the new cardinals. More than 1,000 clergy and laity were gathered in the dining hall. But despite their numbers, there was a remarkable hush over the throng.

Across the city, in a consistorial hall at the Apostolic Palace of the Vatican, Pope John strode briskly in and took his place on his throne while a functionary cried out the historic *"Extra omnes,"* the warning for all persons except cardinals to leave.

The Pope then listed the names of the 23 cardinals he proposed to elevate. He asked the traditional question, *"Quod vobis videtur?"* meaning "What do you think of it?"

The assembly of cardinals promptly rose and each removed his skullcap as a sign of homage to the Pope and assent to his selections. Thus, the Sacred College was automatically increased to an unprecedented 74, from nine different countries.

Back at the North American College, the throng waited more than two hours for the official word. Although the three cardinal-designates wore sober expressions, a break in the tension came when a news photographer came in to take their pictures.

"I hope," commented Cardinal Cicognani, "you title these pictures 'hopeful anticipation.' "

A few moments later, his brother, Gaetano Cardinal Cicognani, came in from the secret consistory and embraced all three waiting prelates.

However, formal notification was necessary so the trio went into the dining hall through a passageway formed by young seminarians. They took their places on three separate chairs, each situated on a 12-foot Persian rug. Cardinal Cicognani, as senior prelate, was in the center.

"I have a letter for his Eminence."

With these words, Richard Cushing was handed a "bi-glietto," a note of the glad tidings, by a messenger from the Papal Secretary of State. It meant that he was to share with the Pope the burdens of governing an international spiritual kingdom of 500,000,000 Roman Catholics.

There was a stir among the clergy and laity. The purple of the cardinals' robes, each adorned with gold crucifixes, blended with the colorful vestments of church dignitaries and the clothes of lay observers.

Bishop Jeremiah Minihan accepted the biglietto addressed to Cardinal Cushing and read it aloud.

Behind the first messenger came a second, bearing the papal decree from the Apostolic Chancery. This was accepted and read by the Cardinal's long-time friend and one-time secretary, Bishop Wright. As it was read, Richard Cushing's face was a study in sober humility.

A third messenger arrived from the office of the Vatican master of ceremonies, with a proclamation that the red hat would be bestowed on the new cardinals three days hence. It was read by the messenger, Monsignor Salvatore Capo-feri, the Italian rector-in-theory of Santa Susanna Church in Rome of which Cardinal Cushing would be titualr head.

The two other cardinals from the United States also received their three notices and all listened to brief remarks of congratulation from Monsignor Capoferi. After each had expressed his sincere gratitude and his filial devotion to the Pontiff whom each recognized as the personal vicar of Christ on earth, the ceremony was ended and the guests pressed forward to declare their homage and joy.

It was in keeping with ancient tradition for Richard Cushing to become titular head of one of Rome's ancient churches as a cardinal. The one to which he was assigned was named in honor of Santa Susanna, the niece of an early Pope, who died a martyr. His appointment to the Church of Santa Susanna also emphasized the difference between his being an archbishop and being a cardinal. As a cardinal, he became a prince of the church, a designation that placed him in the Pope's Council, a group that nominally advises the Pontiff and from whose ranks succeeding Popes are customarily elected. The title is more of a political one than an ecclesiastical one, since he was elevated by John to be a part of his administration, and would hold the title for life. It would have no direct bearing on his duties as Archbishop of Boston, except as papal recognition of the importance of the see and the qualities of its administrator. He also retained another little-publicized title of Metropolitan of the See of Boston, a designation with Eastern Rite connotations recognizing his authority over the bishops of the subordinate dioceses of the New England Province.

As titular head of the Church of Santa Susanna, Cardinal Cushing contributes to its upkeep. Its routine affairs are under the administration of the Paulist Fathers, whom the Cardinal brought to Boston in 1945 to establish the Catholic Information Center overlooking Boston Common. Significantly, the Paulists introduced a succession of progressive cardinals to speak on the Vatican Council at public lectures in 1963 and 1964. As Cardinal, Richard Cushing entertained these prelates at his residence in the period just before he took a leading role at the third session of the Vatican Council, which came to grips with such issues as religious liberty, redefinition of the role of bishops and full exoneration of the Jews of responsibility for the Crucifixion.

On December 18, 1958, Richard James Cushing from East Third Street, South Boston, stood before the Throne of St. Peter with the other new princes of the church to receive their red hats from Pope John. It was a ceremony dating from the ages, but with innovations that would have startled the ancient prelates. Television cameras stared down into the Basilica, along with motion picture and still cameras. Yet the words that the sound equipment recorded were the same as those intoned centuries ago.

The Boston delegation had been in place for an hour when the Kleig lights in St. Peter's were turned on at 8 A.M. In the apse were nobles of the Papal Court, members of the diplomatic corps of all nations. Special guests and the press were in raised stands above twoscore cameras along the base of the huge pillars.

As silver trumpets blared, the Pope was carried in, surrounded by nobles and Swiss guards. He was wearing a gold miter and the flowing red cope of his office.

Cardinal Cushing was the tenth to receive his red hat from hands of the Pope, kneeling while the Pontiff placed it on his head. Pope John said:

"By this you are to understand that you must show yourself fearless even to the shedding of blood, in making our Holy Faith respected, in securing peace for our Christian people and in promoting the welfare of the Roman Church. In the name of the Father and of the Son and of the Holy Ghost. Amen."

A tremendous wave of applause and rousing cheers greeted the Boston cardinal's approach to the throne. A heavy downpour had begun during the ceremony and held most of the crowd inside for some time after it was over.

At a reception by the Boston pilgrims later at the North American College, Cardinal Cushing disclosed that the Pope had thanked him as he kissed the Papal fisherman's ring after receiving the red hat. He said the Pope beamed and exclaimed, "Ah, Cushing! Boston! Ah! Ah!"

The Cardinal also displayed a consistorial ring that he had received during his stay. He explained at the reception that it was "one that you get when assigned a titular church. It symbolizes the authority of the Holy See and the fact that I'm a Roman priest and bishop in charge of a Roman church. When I am in Rome I wear it."

He also dug into his pocket and produced a second ring with an aquamarine surrounded by diamonds that he would wear at home. When it came time for Richard Cushing to make a few remarks to his group, he said, "I'm glad I can speak in the vernacular because I have had a hard time making myself understood in Latin over here.

"These honors cannot make me work any harder," he said, but expressed hope they would prove an inspiration and encouraging to the people of the Boston Archdiocese.

"I have died six deaths during the past week," he went on. "Temperamentally and psychologically I do not feel equipped for the honors which have come to me."

After expressing his gratitude to those who had come with him, the Cardinal voiced hope that he could do more for the Church Universal.

"We should ride on the deck of the bark of St. Peter, not in the boiler room," he told the Bostonians. "We should expose ourselves to the dangers of work and propagate the faith. The only way to keep faith alive is to propagate it."

During the reception, Monsignor Di Roccagiovanni, a papal messenger, arrived to deliver Cardinal Cushing's galero, a special broad-brimmed red hat that he was to wear that day only. On his death, it will be placed on his catafalque. Then, it will be hung from the vaulted ceiling of the

Cathedral of the Holy Cross in Boston, beside that of Cardinal O'Connell, until it disintegrates.

Three days after the ceremony in St. Peter's, the new Boston cardinal alighted at Logan International Airport at Boston. This time, the temperature was 10 degrees above zero. After a few moments of posing for pictures, Cardinal Cushing exclaimed, "Let's go inside before we all catch pneumonia!"

Cardinal Cushing was wearing the bright scarlet traveling robes of his new office. On the plane with him were 54 pilgrims. The prelate said to those who could hear, "These people are fatigued. So am I. I am going to say the ten o'clock mass for them at the chapel here so they can fulfill their religious obligation today.

"I am happy to be home. I was the happiest priest in the world before this ecclesiastical honor was conferred on me. The higher you go, the more difficult it becomes and the heavier the crosses you have to carry," he went on.

"But I'm sure that I'll be able to do everything required of me and at the same time carry my cross with patience and resignation. I don't propose to change. I'll go along as usual striving to serve all people."

The Cardinal posed for a while for the Boston news photographers, chatting all the time with the reporters.

"The Pope is a very kindly and humble man," he told them. "I hope I'm not being irreverent, if I suggest somewhat of my type, in that he likes people, and likes to be of service to people."

Cardinal Cushing said he characterized the Pontiff as "Good Pope John," and commented that he wouldn't be surprised if the appellation stuck.

He told the reporters that the plane had stopped off at

Shannon, Ireland, on the trip from Rome, and that he was asleep as it touched down.

"Imagine an Irishman sleeping over Ireland!" he commented.

On hand in the cold were his two sisters, Mrs. Francis and Mrs. Pierce, and two nephews, Father Francis and Richard Francis. It took a group of state and Boston police, forming an arm-linking cordon, to make way for the prelate to Our Lady of the Airways Chapel. Inside, more than 300 persons had packed themselves.

As he was about to enter, Cardinal Cushing spotted Sister Malachy, mother provincial of the Franciscan Missionary Sisters of Mary. As she stopped to kiss his ring, the prelate asked, "Do you recognize me in this outfit?"

It was a few moments before the scheduled 10 A.M. time for Sunday mass at the chapel, so the Cardinal said, "You see, even a cardinal has to obey the instruction of his pastor." And he waited until the Rev. John D. Hausman, chaplain of the chapel, signaled the hour had arrived to begin the mass.

Afterward, when as many as wished had come to the altar rail to kiss the new cardinal's ring, he was driven to his residence where he rested for the remainder of the day. But at evening, on the scheduled program, he recited the Rosary for the first time since his departure.

In spite of his persistent overwork, there was no particular concern over the Cardinal's health for several years. In July 1959 it was announced that the Cardinal was being hospitalized for treatment of his chronic asthma and a very painful case of shingles. He remained there for five days. When he flew to Rome the following October to attend ceremonies marking the centennial of the North American College, he told friends he planned to stop over on his return trip for four days of rest and medical examination at Our Lady of Lourdes Hospital in Ireland, to which the Cardinal had recently donated a wing. He sent back a message that the physical checkup turned out as well as could be expected and that the people of the Boston Archdiocese were not to worry.

But two months later the Cardinal suffered two fainting spells on the same day in Kansas City, Missouri. Outside the banquet hall where he was to make an appearance, he had a spell of dizziness but managed to overcome it. But at the banquet table, listening to the preliminary addresses, he turned white and fell forward in a semiconscious state. A physician was unable to find a pulse; and a stretcher and resuscitator were brought in. A priest stood by to administer last rites. But the Cardinal recovered, waved away the physician and priest, and shortly afterward delivered a twenty-minute address.

In January, 1960, Cardinal Cushing was ordered to bed with a severe case of laryngitis; and when he could not shake it off was again admitted to St. Elizabeth's Hospital.

For nearly a year he remained in good health, then suffered a heavy cold followed by an attack of influenza. After he insisted on visiting the naval aircraft carrier *Lake Champlain* in Boston Navy Yard and strolling on the deck without an overcoat, greeting the crew, he was again back in bed. Shortly thereafter he was returned to St. Elizabeth's with symptoms of stomach ulcers. There he was put on a milk and cream diet and given blood transfusions, though he kept on working in his room at the hospital, where he remained until March 12. Upon his release he was admonished to make no public appearances, but he addressed his

flock editorially in the *Pilot* to thank them for their prayers
and comfort, and indicated that his diet for bleeding ulcers
would have to continue. That he could continue his activities as leader of his archdiocese and as cardinal, his travels,
and his increased efforts relating to the Vatican Ecumenical
Council is a phenomenon no one has been able to explain.

Even after he had been designated a cardinal, Cushing
asked Pope John to be allowed to pass up the honor to become a missionary. Pope John turned down his request,
but in 1960 gave him an opportunity to go out to his fa-
vored missionary field, South America, by naming him a
papal delegate to a national eucharistic congress in Peru. It
was like sending a chafing armchair strategist into the front
lines. Cushing had listened for years to reports of South
America from visiting missionaries. It had inspired him to
found the Society of St. James the Apostle to encourage
priests to go into the mission field in Latin America.

The Boston prelate found himself tied to a schedule that
reminded him of home. Although the Congress ran only
from August 25 to August 29, he spent two weeks in Peru,
speaking and visiting places daily. One of his trips was to
Curahussi, a remote parish high in the Andes mountains.
He was accompanied on a flight from Lima by President
and Mrs. Manuel Prado of Peru, who told him, "What
Peru needs is more of your Boston priests." In the tiny village, Cardinal Cushing found Father David Kelly, a native
of Arlington, Massachusetts, the first of a number of Bostonians who had accepted his call for missionary vocations.

On his return home, Cardinal Cushing said he found evidence of Peruvian gratitude for American aid, but that at
the same time he had also found evidence of considerable
Communist activity and pleaded for more missionary

priests to combat the Red menace to Christianity. In citing the need for at least 100,000 priests, the prelate said, "In some cases, people may be visited by a Communist agent every day but see a priest once a month or once every two months, or perhaps a few times a year. The people are very religious but they are uninformed. There are hundreds of thousands who have no priest to guide them."

The Peruvian venture so impressed the Pope that he sent Cardinal Cushing to Bolivia on a similar assignment in 1961. In one of his addresses, the Boston prelate told one audience, "We cannot do much for Latin America until someone succeeds in convincing rich capitalists to distribute their possessions. A Communist dictator will be able to do it, but by pointing a gun at their heads." He returned to Boston from that trip with a warning that unless legislative changes were made in the social order in Peru and Bolivia, both nations would fall to Communism.

Although Cushing has been continually thwarted in his wish to become a missionary priest in Latin America, and his activities on behalf of that area have received far less publicity than his public appearances and his functions as Archbishop of Boston, the Church in Latin America has been one of the most important preoccupations of his life. Over the years he has quietly raised millions of dollars for the Society of St. James the Apostle. The magnitude of that work, his interest in Latin America, and his phenomenal gifts as a fund raiser were to be spectacularly revealed in 1963 when he was called on to help raise money for the ransom of exiled Cubans taken prisoner by Fidel Castro's forces in the abortive Bay of Pigs invasion, April 11, 1961.

One night, shortly before Christmas, 1962, the Cardinal received a telephone call from the Attorney General of the United States. He needed to raise $2,900,000 in ransom money to satisfy the demands of Premier Fidel Castro of Cuba. The money had to come from private sources, since the Government of the United States could not deal offi- cially with Castro in matters arising from the attempted in- vasion. Nevertheless, time was short. Could his Eminence help? The prelate, who had known the Attorney General as Bobby Kennedy of the Hyannis Port family of Kennedys as a baby, said he was sure that something could be done if the President's younger brother could call back in an hour.

In the meantime, the Cardinal began dialing numbers all over the archdiocese. And when an assistant attorney general made a return call from Washington, he was as- sured that $1,000,000 would be forthcoming from Boston, provided that the donor remain anonymous. It would be raised by the end of January.

When Castro actually began releasing prisoners, Attor- ney General Kennedy made known some of the details of the deal. He said that $1,000,000 of the amount had been raised by a single donor. Immediately, rumors began flying. It seemed logical that someone like Joseph P. Kennedy, the family patriarch, would have that much money readily at call.

The Boston *Globe* said that there had been hints among Republicans of their making an issue of the ransom money and of possible demands of a Congressional investigation. One rumor even suggested that the money came from a racketeer. It was also said that 25 to 30 individuals raised half of the money and banks agreed to lend the rest.

But shortly afterward, in the January 11, 1963, issue of the *Pilot,* Cardinal Cushing, in a characteristically ram- bling explanation, identified himself as the donor of the major contribution in order to set at rest reports that the money had come from "sources with which I had no identification."

At a press conference shortly after the *Pilot* went to press the Cardinal flatly asserted, "I did not receive any of the money from Joseph Kennedy, I do not believe that Joseph Kennedy was aware of my fund raising for the ransom."

Premier Castro demanded $2,900,000 for the immediate release of 60 of the more seriously wounded of 1,113 prisoners. Before the situation had been resolved, the ante had risen to include $53,000,000 in drugs and medicine, and the discovery of Soviet missiles on the island had brought the nation to the brink of war.

The Cardinal described his part in the raising of ransom money in this way:

"I received a telegram on December 28, 1962. It came from the Cuban Families' Committee. It was an invitation to attend the reception given by the President of the United States to the 'Cuban Freedom Fighters' in Miami, who had been recently liberated from imprisonment.

"Prior to that time, I was identified with the original committee that was to collect the multimillion-dollar ransom price for these prisoners. This committee never formally functioned and to my knowledge it collected no funds.

"Then I became one of the sponsors of, and advisers to, the Cuban Families' Committee consisting of relatives of those taken prisoner at the time of the abortive invasion in April, 1961, of their native land at the Bay of Pigs. Quietly I contacted a host of benefactors who have helped me to collect a million dollars and more each year during the past five years for the Missionary Society of St. James the Apostle, which I founded, and for other projects helpful to the Catholic Church in Latin America.

"These benefactors assured me of their support for the liberation of the prisoners captured in a hopeless effort to reclaim the land of their birth.

"The object of the Society of St. James the Apostle is to recruit diocesan priests from the United States, Ireland and other English-speaking countries, who would volunteer to go to Latin America and serve poor people who had inherited the faith of their forebears but who had no priests to work among them. The secondary object of this society is to refute the promises and propaganda of false prophets. For this latter objective hundreds of thousands of pieces of literature, including 200,000 of the Spanish edition of our booklet, 'Questions and Answers on Communism,' have been distributed. I assumed all responsibility for the cost and printing of these booklets.

"At the present time the Society of St. James numbers about a hundred priest volunteers who with the permission of their respective bishops are now in charge of parishes in Bolivia, Peru and Ecuador which otherwise would be without priests.

"Through this missionary society I have also collected and allocated over one million dollars annually to bishops in Latin America for schools, churches, modern seminaries for the training of future priests and other good works which would help missionaries to be zealous apostles of Christ and ambassadors of good will for the United States.

"Those identified with the liberation of the Cuban prisoners who were captured in a hopeless attempt to recapture their native land were well aware of my activities in behalf of the Church and social justice in Latin America. When, therefore, it was necessary to collect $2,900,000 in addition to the millions of dollars' worth of food and medicines a few days before Christmas for the release of these prisoners,

I again assumed an active part in the collecting of that fund.

"I immediately pledged the sum of $1,000,000 to be collected by me prior to the end of January. Like many others, I wanted the prisoners home with their loved ones before Christmas Day. The sum I promised was given by donors in many parts of the United States and in some parts of Latin America. They are all interested in the many good works for which I accept responsibility in Latin American countries.

"Some of this money was already available as a result of gifts received when I became one of the sponsors of the appeal represented by the Committee of Cuban Families for the release of their loved ones from the prisons of Cuba.

"I wanted no publicity about this pledge because I was only a voice appealing for those who could not appeal for themselves. The donors responded in the spirit of Christmas, with the understanding that their money would be returned if the ransom sum could not be raised. I worked day and night in the same spirit and through person to person contacts I have fulfilled my pledge.

"This in brief is the story of the anonymous gift of $1,000,000 from a so-called 'mysterious donor.' It must now be told because I am receiving telephone calls from those identified with certain media of communications, indicative of rumors crediting this gift as coming from sources with which I have no identification. I alone am responsible for the collection of this extraordinary sum. The credit, however, belongs to my co-workers and benefactors in the United States and Latin America who have supported my apostolic works in the most crucial area of the western hemisphere.

"In my opinion the most effective bond of unity capable

of uniting the multitudes of Latin America against the advance of Communism is their common Catholic Faith. It is appropriate and fitting, therefore, for a Catholic prelate of the United States to have a part in the liberation of the 'Cuban Freedom Fighters' who love their country and the 'Faith of their fathers.' "

In expanding his explanation at the press conference, Cardinal Cushing disclosed that he had $200,000 on hand when Robert Kennedy called on him for help.

"I was saving the money until I was sure it was used for the purposes intended," he said. "It was my reserve."

The additional $800,000 was raised through small contributions, the Cardinal told reporters, asserting that there had been no substantial contribution from any one source, including foundations. The largest gift, $1,000, came from a source he declined to identify.

Overall contributions from wealthy persons in Latin America had been less than he had hoped for, said the Cardinal. He commented, "There are some tremendously wealthy people in Latin America, but they haven't been trained to give."

Cushing's duties as archbishop and cardinal do not require the strenuous effort that he has devoted to Latin America; but it has remained consistent through the years despite the demands of his own archdiocese. In the summer of 1964, he made a third trip to South America, this time on his own. In Peru he gave courage to struggling priests, preached until his voice was exhausted, blessed buildings that he had financed, and poured hundreds of gallons of milk into mugs for orphans in institutions he visited. The Peruvians were overwhelmed by the American tourist manner of the Bostonian. He would go into a store and ask the proprietor how much it would cost for enough ice cream to fill the gaggle of youngsters who were trailing after him. If the store owner mentioned the equivalent of ten or twelve United States dollars, the Cardinal would plunk down twenty-five and say, "All right, give them the second round tomorrow!"

CHAPTER XI

Corruption and Justice

ABOUT the time that the Vatican was becoming condi-
tioned to the political climate of the twentieth century
under Pope John XXIII, the Archdiocese of Boston, under
its new cardinal, Richard J. Cushing, was reaping a bitter
harvest. Not only the archdiocese, but the entire Commonwealth of Massachusetts was rocked by what Federal Judge
Charles E. Wyzanski, Jr., for one called "a network of corruption."

The end of World War II had thrown the nation back
on its own economic resources, many of them government-
controlled as the result of the massive legislative program
undertaken by President Franklin D. Roosevelt, an Episcopalian, to combat the Great Depression of the nineteen-thir-
ties.

Sweeping social legislation had taken over the bread-
and-butter tasks once performed by the old political bosses
of the James Michael Curley, Frank Hague and Frank Pren-
dergast school of benevolent despots trading Christmas
baskets and economic influence for ballots. In their places

were social welfare bureaus, staffed by an increasing army of public jobholders.

In Massachusetts, with the decline and fall of the Brahmin political empire had risen a new breed of smart, second- and third-generation Irish Catholic politicians. Schooled in the war tradition of "taking care" of one's constituents in election years as well as in off years, they had forged the Democratic Party into a force that figuratively marched on City Hall and conquered it.

Dealing with such day-to-day problems as food on the table, a weekly pay envelope, housing and workmen's compensation, for example, the Democratic Party had an almost ironclad formula for appealing to the workingman, who, around Boston, meant great masses of Irish Catholics.

Although Republicans, during their heyday, had enacted many social reforms that made Massachusetts a leader in the field of such things as child labor laws and forbidding the use of women on third shifts, they lost the initiative to Roosevelt, a New York brand of Brahmin, in 1932. But the Massachusetts Irish had already gotten their backs up in the bitter Presidential campaign of 1928, when Al Smith, the Irish Catholic governor of New York, carried the state in his unsuccessful try as the Democratic national standard-bearer. And no Republican carried Massachusetts again until Dwight D. Eisenhower turned the trick in 1952 and 1956.

None of this was lost on Richard Cushing, who, but for the toe of Father Toomey's boot, might have joined the army of political revolt that marched out of South Boston, captured City Hall and laid siege to the State House. During the quarter century following his elevation to bishop, Richard Cushing saw the governorship seesaw between the two parties.

In the World War II years, a Republican Leverett Saltonstall could win election to three straight terms. But in the next sixteen years, beginning in 1946, the post swung back and forth between the two parties. And of the three governors who managed to be elected to more than a single term, two were Democrats.

At the same time, Democrats gradually began to turn the tide in the legislature, as well as in the state constitutional offices below governor. The office of Speaker of the House fell into Democratic hands in 1954 and the Presidency of the Senate in 1958.

Through this period, the political lineups of the two parties were almost entirely made up of Yankee Protestant names under the Republican label and Irish Catholics under the Democratic. In the 1948 election, when Harry S. Truman confounded the experts by winning the Presidency, the Democratic National Committeewoman from Massachusetts was moved to note that "that nice little Baptist man, Mr. Truman, won't campaign on Sunday."

The *Pilot* was moved to publish an editorial, "A Plague on Both Your Houses," in noting the rigidity of both parties in naming slates. From then on, the two parties got the message. And in the continuing rise to power of the Democrats, Italians got their chance in the sun, although they still were Catholics. The Republicans eventually elected an Italian Catholic governor and a Protestant Negro attorney general.

But the legislature fell, like ripe fruit, into the Democratic basket. Through this period of travail, a burgeoning and mobile population, spreading out into the suburbs and winning economic gains that enabled it to have summer homes, as well, demanded more and better highways. And with the lifting of wartime restrictions on materials, the age of the bulldozer dawned in 1948.

An inept Republican administration failed that year to put across a highway bond issue, but with Governor Dever in office for four years beginning in 1949 the rush was on.

It still took some Republican support to gain two-thirds votes for multimillion-dollar bond issues, and wheeling and dealing for that support meant a share of largesse to G.O.P. collaborators.

The state department of public works became the fountainhead of much of the flood of funds. There were land damage settlements, "finders' " fees for bringing buyer and seller together along rights of way, fat contracts, contract performance bonds, insurance and a host of other necessary facets of the operation.

And as the highways began to spread across the land, with divided strips and bridge embankments that needed to be sown with grass, and dual lanes that needed snow-plowing according to the seasons, a year-round business in maintenance developed. This led to fees for renting equipment to the state, particularly if one had connections.

The general economic boom called for new outlets for spending, and among the side effects of it all were illegal gambling and income tax evasions.

In January, 1960, the Federal Bureau of Roads announced that it had stopped payment of right-of-way acquisition costs to Massachusetts because of assumed misuse of these payments. The amount involved more than $9,000,-000.

Judge Wyanski, presiding at an income tax evasion trial, issued a "clarion call" to combat what he saw as a coiled malignancy throughout the commonwealth. He spared no one, including the bar and the press.

Suddenly, Massachusetts found itself in the national spotlight as visiting writers moved in to tell what they had found for the benefit of nationally circulated newspapers and magazines.

As the first wave of indictments were returned by Federal grand juries, it was obvious that Republicans were among the beneficiaries of graft. But Democrats were in overwhelming power in Massachusetts and they took the brunt of the blame.

For his pastoral letter for the Lenten season of 1961, Cardinal Cushing produced a 40-page dissertation on "Moral Values and the American Society," in which he lashed out at corruption in high places. It was mandatory for parish priests to preach on the subject in their churches.

"We cannot expect to provide a wholesome social environment unless each of us assumes some responsibility for the right ordering of our government at every level, from the lowest to the highest," the prelate asserted.

The right to vote, he said, "entails the obligation to vote for those best fitted to serve the community, not for those from whom we hope to gain some selfish and purely personal advantage."

And, he went on, "when public officials are dishonest they are false to the oath of office which an enduring Christian tradition requires them to pronounce.

"When public officials who have proved themselves to be dishonest are returned to office again and again, the voter emblazons before the world his own indifference to the moral law," Cardinal Cushing declared. "This is a matter of gravest scandal. It is plain that the voting citizen in such a situation encourages the spread of corruption and is himself a kind of 'partner in crime.'

"I cannot find language strong enough to bear the burden of moral judgment that must fall upon those individuals who poison politics with dishonesty and corruption. These are genuine subversives who turn to wickedness the good order of society. When we hear murmurs of graft and bribery, of 'payoffs' and 'grabs,' we know these charges are not the products of the imaginations of fanciful people; they take their course in a sordid reality which decent society cannot afford to tolerate," said the Cardinal.

Sermons in Protestant churches followed a similar pattern and there was much public hand wringing. But crime and corruption continued to flourish in the rich soil that had been prepared over a period of years. An indifferent electorate returned the same faces to the legislature, causing the tar to be splashed on dedicated lawmakers indiscriminately. One Boston legislator, convicted of larceny in connection with failure of his family contracting firm to complete a sidewalk contract, was easily re-elected while sitting in jail.

In early June of 1961, the Columbia Broadcasting System set up a camera in a vacant apartment in Boston's Back Bay. It was trained for three days on a key shop across the street. During the period, several hundred persons walked in and out of the shop. None carried keys that were visible. But among the customers were ten Boston policemen, in uniform.

At one point, a man who apparently was a key shop employee came out and burned a couple of handfuls of slips of paper in a small metal barrel, while a policeman looked idly on.

Then, on September 29, the camera again was in place when Federal agents brought in from other states raided the shop and arrested eight persons on charges of booking horses.

The films taken by the camera were shown on a nationally televised documentary, "CBS Reports: Biography of a Bookie Joint," on November 30. The show was blacked out in Boston because of the cases pending against the eight men.

Although the program described how illegal gambling was a national disease, the Boston key shop served as a revealing example of the widespread breakdown in lay enforcement and public morals.

The effect on the city was electric. But rather than expressing much dismay over the moral issues involved, the general reaction was one of shock that Boston had been selected for the leading role. The President of the Chamber of Commerce, a suburbanite, commented that it was "most unfortunate and in a sense unfair in view of the vast national establishment of off-track bookie shops."

Cardinal Cushing was furious. He showed up at the annual Boston Policeman's Ball in the Boston Garden a few nights later and asserted that the city had been "betrayed."

"Gambling exists everywhere, and no one can deny it," he cried. "The United States Army wouldn't be a sufficient law enforcement body to stop people from gambling."

Although as an archbishop he had once expressed his opposition to racetracks, he now declared, "In my theology, gambling itself is not a sin any more than to take a glass of beer or of hard liquor is a sin. It's the abuse that makes gambling evil or drinking intoxicating liquor a sin."

The angry prelate said he had not seen the program, nor was he interested in seeing it. But he asserted that "whoever is behind it owes the city of Boston an apology."

Later, the Cardinal confided that he was moved to express himself publicly to reassure honest policemen and their wives, most of them Irish Catholics, that he appreciated that they were trying to do their jobs.

But Dwight S. Strong, executive secretary of the New England Citizens Crime Commission, Inc., a voluntary agency that had been created from the wreckage of the blue-nose watch and Ward Society of the Roaring Twenties, expressed a widely held view that "for too long we have been sweeping under the rug these conditions and now perhaps the public will be awakened to the situation."

The legislature awakened by censuring Rep. Harrison Chadwick, a Republican from suburban Winchester, who had appeared on the documentary as a commentator and had stated that some Massachusetts lawmakers were "actively involved with bookmakers."

While Mr. Chadwick could not produce firm enough evidence to convince the legislative committee that heard him, it was not long after that the capitol police raided the legislative document room and found that it was doing flourishing business in booking horses and numbers.

The legislative aide in charge of the room was discharged, although he said he was only "an amateur handicapper," who had never registered a bet in his life. But he said he knew a dozen legislators who were steady customers with local bookies. The Republican Administration made a perfunctory investigation of the incident. But by the same token, the Democratic-controlled Senate had applied a whitewash to the Department of Public Works after having showed what might be done by cleaning house in the Metropolitan District Commission, a state agency concerned with parks, highways and sewers in the Boston area.

Nevertheless, the airing of the bookie scandal had the

effect of creating a public awareness of the commonwealth's bad image, more than any moralizing by religious leaders in pulpits of all faiths.

Governor John A. Volpe, a Republican who had ridden into office as an avowed crusader during a wave of public soul-searching in 1960, was finally stirred into action late in his single two-year term. He led a campaign to establish a special crime commission of seven persons, none of whom was a legislator. The commission finally went to work after Mr. Volpe had been narrowly defeated for a second term by Endicott Peabody, an Episcopalian, and the first Protestant Democrat to be elected governor in thirty years.

The commission flushed out enough evidence, despite foot dragging by some witnesses, to present a post of indictments. Then, suddenly, after the commission had handed down 26 indictments in one fell swoop, Cardinal Cushing went on a radio discussion program on Station WEEI, Boston, and lashed out at the commission.

In answer to a question by Paul Benzaquin, the director of the show, as to whether he thought the commission had outlived its usefulness, Cardinal Cushing said that it was "too bad the commission was ever set up."

Apart from normal investigatory channels, the Cardinal asserted, the keen competition among men and women striving for recognition and election should be enough to pinpoint dishonesty and scandal. Those, and "other sources of knowledge, should be all that was necessary for getting information about wrongdoing and a demand that the wrongdoers be banished from public life.

"If there was a crime commission in every state," he said, "the state of Massachusetts probably would have a better image than any other state."

Scoring those who he said preached that Boston and Mas-

sachusetts were crime-ridden at every level, the prelate declared, "Somehow the people of the state and the city
haven't enough loyalty to go about eliminating evil—real
or imagined—without portraying them as places where
crime and corruption are rampant."

Cardinal Cushing defended the role of the Church in
exposing corruption or a breakdown in morality, asserting
that its approach should be positive and never one of condemnation.

"You hear a lot of rumors, cheap talk with regard to
those things," he said. "It is one thing to indict a man; it is
another to prove the indictment.

"It is one thing to preach a positive message; it is another thing entirely—something we should never do—to
condemn people even though they are guilty, because our
mission is one of mercy," said the Cardinal.

Several prominent Republicans had been among those
in the group of 26 indicted, and while their friends were in
agreement with the Cardinal to some extent, the general
reaction was one of bewilderment, particularly in view of
his 1961 Lenten pastoral letter. It seemed another example
of the Cardinal's contradictory temperament. But one explanation might be that, while the Cardinal could be stern
in laying down the moral law to his flock, the Boston Irishman was quick to spring to the defense of his own people
when they were unwarrantably attacked by outsiders.

CHAPTER XII

The Ecumenical Council

ONE of the first acts of Pope John XXIII on ascending the Throne of Peter was to announce his intention of calling an Ecumenical Council.

The Council was to be the Church's 21st since the Council of Nicaea in 325, and it was the second, after 92 years, to be held in Rome. When someone in a visiting group asked the Pope why he felt moved to take such a step, he led them to a window, drew aside the drapes and said with a mischievous smile and in a gentle tone, "You see, that is why I called the Council, to let fresh air come into the Church."

For a prelate who had been letting intermittent blasts of fresh air into his archdiocese for a decade and a half, it was a congenial plan. Cardinal Cushing, upon succeeding Cardinal O'Connell as archbishop, had aired out the chancery, established direct contact with his people rather than addressing them through the cumbersome and often obscure majesty of the church machinery. He treated liturgy with reverence but also with a confident familiarity, as well as with a South Boston accent, that suggested that it was intended to convey rather than obscure the essence of religion. In matters of dogma he had shown a tactful consideration for the views of non-Catholics, especially in the embarrassing case of Father Feeney, and he had not been heavy-handed in interpreting theology. He was not, in fact, given to scholarly theological pronouncements, relying more on his intuition of an immediate human situation when he was required to speak or act for the Church. Despite occasional conflicts with them, he was on notably good terms with the Protestant and Jewish communities; and he had achieved this good fellowship without ever backing down on the necessity and the right of Catholics to profess and practice their own faith. Among American prelates, Cardinal Cushing was one of those most likely to favor renewal in the Church for the sake of strengthening the Church as well as its ties with the world community.

Although he did not live to see the full program carried out, Pope John was on hand to take a vigorous part in the first session that finally opened on October 11, 1962, three years after the call. Among the 2,600 prelates on hand was the Cardinal Archbishop of Boston. His flock, back home, had been well briefed in what to expect from the Council by pastoral letter, speeches and newspaper stories under his personal by-line.

Principally, Cardinal Cushing warned his people not to expect miracles.

"The greatest thing to come from the Council is a second spring for the Church," he told students at Boston College. "It can erase apathy and increase personal sanctity."

On the eve of his departure, Cardinal Cushing was tendered a bon voyage party at Blinstrub's, where he had held so many Thanksgiving dinners for the aged. This time, instead of the usual good-natured joshing, the Cardinal seriously expressed hope that the Council would "spread among Catholics, Protestants, Jews, atheists and Communists, love for the dignity of man as a person.

"I do not want Catholics disliking Protestants or Jews or atheists or Communists and I do not want them to dislike us for any reason of our belief."

More than a hundred well-wishers were on hand at the Boston airport to see the prelate take off for Rome on October 8. But three youngsters from the Kennedy Memorial Hospital stole the show. Jean Mackey, three years old, whispered, "I'll pray for you." Teddy Judge, six, leaned from his wheelchair and kissed the Cardinal on the cheek. Barbara Schwartz, eight, followed him around on her crutches whenever he moved from group to group saying farewell.

Cardinal Cushing told the well-wishers that the Council would represent a step toward the unity of all Christians. But he counseled, "Of course no one expects any unity of Christianity at this time, but we must become united as children of God. We should recognize the rights of all people to worship in the manner they see fit. Such unity would be good for the welfare of the community, the welfare of our commonwealth and indeed the welfare of our country."

As he had in the past, the prelate reiterated that "actual unity will come in God's good time, perhaps at the end of the world, but in the meanwhile, we must learn to love one another in the hope of there being one fold, one shepherd."

On the day before the opening of the Council, Boston learned that its cardinal archbishop again had pleaded to resign and devote his remaining years to missionary work in Latin America. He was turned down by an old friend, Amleto Cicognani, now a cardinal and Vatican Secretary of State. He was told that he was needed in Boston.

Discussing his session with Cardinal Cicognani the next day, Cardinal Cushing merely said, "The Holy See turned it down. There's no comment because there's nothing more to be said about it. It's all over."

The Cardinal was well received in Rome. The influential Rome daily, *Il Messaggero,* described him as "a tall clean man, with the look of a pioneer of the West."

By the end of the month, the Cardinal had returned to Boston, to plunge into his routine of making speeches and raising money. Gradually, he recounted some of his experiences to add to the list of Cushing anecdotes.

To an audience of 700 members of the Holy Name Society, on December 2, 1962, he told this story of the Pope's being concerned for the health of the Boston prelate.

"Are you feeling well?" the Pope asked. "You seem to get thinner and thinner every time I see you."

"I'm feeling as well as can be expected, your Holiness," replied Cardinal Cushing. "But I can't do as much as I'd like to for the poor back in Boston because I have bleeding ulcers."

"Oh, that's too bad," the Pope responded feelingly. "Why don't you take a little bicarbonate of soda before you go to bed at night? I do and it's marvelous."

"Your Holiness," the Cardinal retorted, "thank God you're not infallible when prescribing medicine. That's the worst thing you can take for ulcers!"

At a subsequent dinner, the Cardinal explained that if one of the 2,600 cardinals, patriarchs, archbishops and bishops in St. Peter's Basilica wished to speak at one of the sessions, he had to submit his speech, in Latin, three days in advance.

"It wasn't to be any longer than ten minutes," the prelate said, "but of couse, bishops are like everyone else, some are long-winded and some did speak too long.

"A senior cardinal was elected each day to preside, but as we know, a bishop's only superior is the Pope, so, when the cardinal would rap his gavel to indicate a bishop should stop speaking, they'd just look at him and go right on talking.

"After this had gone on for a few days, the Pope, who had been watching the proceedings over closed-circuit television, sent down word that no more comments would be made on this particular subject unless the speaker had something new to add, and then he had to confine his talk to five minutes.

"As I looked over those 2,600 prelates, most of whom hadn't a chance to speak yet, all I could think of was the power of that man!"

Cardinal Cushing said that his Latin was so deficient that he was lost at the Council, that he lasted only two weeks.

"Even though one might be proficient in Latin—and I never heard a Latin lecture until I went to the Council—if you hear a Frenchman or a German or a Spaniard, especially, talk Latin, you wouldn't know whether he was speaking Chinese or Japanese," the Cardinal said.

The Pontiff gave him permission to return home whenever he wanted, Cardinal Cushing told several audiences. And he added that when the Pope asked him how long he wanted to stay, "I told him I'd better stay three weeks otherwise people would think I had been excommunicated."

"I used to see these bishops and cardinals go out for an hour or so and I wondered where they were going," he once recounted. "I later found out that some of the bishops would get tired and they'd go out to have a cup of coffee— if they had anything else out there I didn't know it because I didn't even see the bars.

"But, in any event, the observers would go out and in a very friendly, fraternal atmosphere they accomplished wonders by breaking down barriers.

"The first I learned about these bars was when a cardinal from Tanganyika, East Africa, congratulated me for sitting there, day after day, listening to those Latin lectures without a coffee break.

"That's the first time I knew these bishops and cardinals were having a little Ecumenical Council of their own.

"I only wish I had heard about them earlier. It was pretty hard sitting there every day for three hours or more and not understand anything they said.

"Most of my priesthood has been spent out on the road getting help for people, raising funds and doing missionary work, not studying Latin."

However, the Cardinal was credited in Rome for having pushed the installation of an electronics system for simultaneous translation of Latin speeches into six languages. It went into operation at the second session, a year later.

The Cardinal once said privately that when he first became archbishop someone suggested that he ought to know tongues other than English and a working knowledge of liturgical Latin. He said that he bought some recordings of French, Italian and other languages and tried for several weeks to master them. Then, he said, he looked into the mirror one morning and exclaimed, "Cush, be yourself!"

But whatever his success with Latin or any other technical matter in Rome, the Cardinal was a changed man on his return. Suddenly, as if shackles had been chopped away, he began to expand his personal views of interfaith cooperation. He announced on November 28, 1962, a few weeks after his return that Augustin Cardinal Bea, a Jesuit who headed the Vatican Secretariat for Christian Unity, would visit New England the following March to lead a series of discussions at the Harvard Divinity School, a training ground for Protestant clergymen, particularly of evangelical disciplines.

Cardinal Cushing said that he and the visiting prelate would speak "anywhere to anyone who will accept us. We will preach our gospel of love and mutual cooperation, a gospel that will respect rights of conscience of all individuals, Jews, Protestants and Catholics.

"In that way, we will create a wonderful climate for the unity of all believers in the Supreme Being. We can leave unity of faith to the providence of Almighty God."

On January 29, 1963, accepting an invitation, the Cardinal appeared on a television program with Bishop James K. Mathews, resident in the New England area of the Methodist Church and president of the Massachusetts Council of Churches. Dean Samuel H. Miller of Harvard Divinity School was moderator. The program was called, "Christian Unity, Dream, Plot or Possibility?"

The Harvard dean noted a radical change in the religious climate and hailed the chance to "talk more freely with less bitterness and misrepresentation and with more open-mindedness and mutual respect than ever before."

Cardinal Cushing said, "I'm all for Catholics being identified with Protestants and Jews, and all others and all kinds in every possible friendly way. Nobody is asking them to deny their faith and they shouldn't be asking anybody to deny their faiths."

"There is now with an increasingly clear voice," said Bishop Mathews, "being heard across what might have been termed an abyss of separation, the cry 'Brother,' and that's a cry that has been directed from both sides, and we find that that abyss perhaps isn't as broad or as deep as we supposed."

It was believed to be the first confrontation of its kind on television. And what it may have lacked in light, in respect of anything deeply theological having been said, it compensated for in warmth of religious climate.

Cardinal Bea arrived in Boston on March 25, and the eighty-one-year-old prelate immediately plunged into a round of ceremonies. The day after his arrival, the Cardinal was awarded an honorary doctorate of civil and canon law by Boston College at a special convocation as part of the Jesuit institution's centennial.

The German-born Vatican diplomat spent three days at Harvard delivering a series known as the Stillman Lectures at a Catholic-Protestant Colloquium. He asserted, "We long to heal the scandalous wounds of separation that prevent all Christians from a perfect internal communion of faith and love, from the external profession of the same faith, from the use of the same sacraments and from the same direction of the same ministry and order."

But he warned, "It stands to reason that overcoming the differences is not a search for compromises. Faith must not be confused with politics."

Cardinal Bea's visit closed with his presence at the Cathedral of the Holy Cross to preside with Cardinal Cushing at a centennial mass in honor of Boston College. His visit had begun an encouraging start of a harvest of goodwill in the archdiocese.

On March 31, 1963, Cardinal Cushing made his announcement about being available for talks in Protestant churches. And five nights later, he addressed the congregation of the Community Church in Westwood, a Boston suburb. The Rev. Dr. Edwin P. Booth, minister emeritus, introduced the prelate, asserting, "The wall that separates us is breached."

Attired in street clericals, the Cardinal discussed the first session of the Vatican Council with the comment, "I am convinced that despite all the scholars gathered over there, your prayers are the greatest contribution to unity."

"There is nothing in the ecumenical movement to get people to change their religious beliefs," the Cardinal told his audience. "The idea is to let us speak to one another, understand one another, love one another and have respect for the conscientious beliefs of one another."

During the rest of 1963, the death of Pope John, a brief stay at the second session of the Council, called by Pope Paul, and the assassination of President Kennedy prevented any further appearances before non-Catholic audiences.

Then, on January 19, the afternoon of Boston's memorial mass for the late President, the Cardinal, after a light lunch, went out to Sudbury to speak at the Methodist church. This time, he was wearing his scarlet biretta and his scarlet-piped black cassock. The first person he met in the foyer was a newspaper reporter whom he did not recognize. He thrust out his hand and said, "My name's Cushing, what's yours?"

The Rev. Blaine Taylor, minister of the church and president of the Sudbury Council of Churches, introduced the Boston visitor. Eight other of the town's clergy were seated in the sanctuary. Among them were the Revs. Robert Hurley and Joseph Birmingham of Our Lady of Fatima Catholic Church.

For more than an hour, Cardinal Cushing drew chuckles and thoughtful attention as he alternately told stories and expounded religious theory. The speech became a basic one for subsequent appearances. Robert L. Johnson, a member of the church, taped the talk, and a week later the Boston *Globe* published an almost complete text that filled a full page of its Sunday editions.

Before settling down into a rambling dissertation on the Council, the prelate gave a brief biography of himself, including his problems in raising money by making speeches. He told his audience:

"The other night I took a taxi from the Statler Hotel where I was making a speech. It was raining—I didn't have any car—I got into a taxi—a Jewish cabby was driving the taxi—I told him where I was going and when I got out he asked, 'Are you the Archbishop?'

"And I said, 'I think I am.'

"He said, 'You're the best rabbi in Boston.'

"He was a smart fellow. He got a $5 tip for that one."

A few moments later, after deprecating his own scholarship in Latin, Cardinal Cushing said he went to visit Pope John to see about returning home.

"I said, 'Are you a theologian, your Holiness? All I know about theology is in Catechism Two.'

"He said, 'Shake hands, you'll never be in trouble!' "

As soon as he returned to Boston from Sudbury, the Cardinal addressed the 50th anniversary banquet of the Catholic Daughters of America, an event that had been postponed because of the President's death. Home briefly to sleep, Cardinal Cushing was off to Chicago the next morning to address the Catholic Inter-American Cooperation Conference.

CHAPTER XIII

Birth Control: Changing Attitudes

PARTLY because of the spirit of renewal within the Church, and partly because of sheer economic necessity, Catholics have begun to question the Church's traditional stand against artificial means of birth control. For a long time, the Church has countenanced the practice of the rhythm method, based on sexual abstention during the period of fertility in the monthly cycle; aside from that it has been rigid in its opposition to any form of contraception and has even fought the dissemination of birth control information among non-Catholics.

Cardinal Cushing had always been a staunch supporter of the Church's position, and took a militant part in defeating repeal of the Massachusetts law forbidding dissemination of birth control information in 1948. Yet in the past two years he has turned about face, asserting in the fall of 1964 that "in no way will I feel it my duty to oppose amendments to the law." Whatever his earlier convictions may have been, the suggestion of Pope Paul that the time might have come for a re-examination of the question has given Cushing the opportunity to express a less intransigent view on the issue.

In April of 1963, an authoritative book on the subject, *The Time Has Come*, was published. The author was Dr. John Rock of Brookline, Massachusetts, a devout Catholic and an internationally known expert on fertility and birth control.

Dr. Rock, then seventy-four years old, was clinical professor emeritus of gynecology at the Harvard Medical School. A graduate of Harvard College and its medical school, he had been associated with the latter since his appointment in 1922 as an assistant in obstetrics.

During a distinguished career in obstetrics and gynecology, Dr. Rock has done exhaustive research in human fertility. He established and for many years directed one of the nation's first fertility clinics at the Free Hospital for Women in his home town of Brookline, a Boston suburb.

But while physicians may treat and prescribe methods for fertility in Massachusetts, the law prohibits the dissemination of birth control information. At the same time, contraceptives are an over-the-counter item in drugstores. Dr. Rock, over the years, frequently has commented on the incongruity of the situation. But it has been more than a decade since the last attempt to repeal the law by referendum.

The last time was in 1948, when the Planned Parenthood League succeeded in placing the issue on the ballot. The measure was bitterly fought by Catholic interests all the way through the legislature. Former Mayor Frederick W. Mansfield of Boston, Archbishop Cushing's legislative agent, appeared in opposition during hearings at the State House.

During the campaign, the Archbishop in an offhand speech accused the proponents of the amendment of having spent more than $50,000 in its behalf. Two days later, Bishop Wright, the prelate's chief speech writer and troubleshooter, issued a statement denying that Archbishop Cushing had specified any exact figure. The Planned Parenthood League, which sponsored the referendum in favor of birth control information, then issued a statement asking "How does the archdiocese maintain its tax-exempt status, when tax laws deny such exemption to groups engaged in influencing legislation?"

The League of Catholic Women undertook a campaign to defeat the referendum. The issue was to be the fourth question on the ballot. A Committee in Opposition to Referendum No. 4 was formed and spent $69,000 on its campaign. The Parenthood forces spent $51,000.

The Sunday before the election, sermons in all Catholic churches were directed against the measure. It was soundly defeated for the second time in six years, the statutory waiting period for a new assault.

At present, Massachusetts and Connecticut alone stand against the legal dissemination of birth control information.

When a hormone pill for contraception was being developed in the 1950s, Dr. Rock was a leader in organizing field trials and conducting the research that declared the final product to be safe.

The pill, a synthetic steroid, was developed by Dr. Gregory Pincus and Dr. M. C. Chang at the Worcester Foundation for Experimental Biology in Shrewsbury, Massachusetts.

Dr. Rock once told an interviewer that he always remembered a visit he made, when he was fourteen years old, with a priest to a town poor farm. As the two drove along in a buggy, the priest said to the boy:

"John, always stick to your conscience. Never let anyone else keep it for you. And I mean anyone else."

In the preface of his book, sixty years later, Dr. Rock wrote:

"With increasing frequency I was disturbed by the realization that the voice of my conscience was not always telling me what the priests of my church kept saying were its dictates regarding human reproductive functioning—what was right and what was wrong in how a person willed, or permitted, or prevented expression of his God-given sexuality."

Dr. Rock presented his book as "a Catholic doctor's proposals to end the battle over birth control." He proposed a national program of research in human fertility and reproduction as an approach to the problem of population. He asserted his belief that techniques of birth control could be developed that would be satisfactory to Catholics and non-Catholics alike. And he suggested a Federal program for research in contraceptive methods, including the rhythm technique.

Although acknowledging there was little possibility of doctrinal agreement on family planning methods then available, the physician-author said that resolution of such differences might come with the refinement of present methods and the development of new approaches.

Dr. Rock expressed hope that the new oral contraceptive, which he described as "the first effective, physiological means of fertility control," would be accepted by the Catholic Church. The pill, said Dr. Rock, prevented reproduction by changing the time sequences of the body's functions. He noted that the church-approved rhythm method depended on the secretion of progesterone from the ovaries, and that since the pills duplicated this action, the physiology involved was identical in both cases.

But Dr. Rock emphasized that the pill could not be the only answer to the population problem; rather, that a variety of techniques was necessary, suitable for use at different social levels and in differing cultures and religions.

A few days before the book was published, Cardinal Cushing wrote a commentary in the *Pilot*. He said he was doing so because Dr. Rock was writing explicitly as a Catholic, "and I am his bishop." The prelate noted that church law required every Catholic writing on a subject pertaining to faith or morality must submit his manuscript to church authority for an imprimatur, or statement by the local bishop that the contents were free from doctrinal or moral error. The Cardinal wrote:

> I regret to observe that Dr. Rock has published his book without such an imprimatur.
>
> Therefore, the opinions on the morality of artificial birth control as presented in the text lack any official approval as authentic Catholic teaching.

However, the Cardinal did not condemn the work out of hand. He continued:

> In this book there is much that is good. The author has presented a detailed and graphic account of the history of the birth control controversy—many times he rightly criticizes the excesses to which some Catholics have gone in this matter. . . .
>
> He presents many cogent arguments for the formation of a public policy on birth control, and some of his sugges-

tions could contribute to the settlement of domestic peace in our pluralistic society.

He makes an eloquent and much-needed plea for Federal grants to perfect the so-called rhythm system so that it might become a means of controlling births which is not only morally acceptable but also scientifically accurate.

Not everything in the book, however, can pass without criticism. It also contains several statements which are theologically incorrect and certainly misleading.

When he speaks on the formation of the Catholic conscience he fails to take into consideration the true complexity of this problem and so commits in the field of theology the same mistake he urges, against the theologians in the field of reproductive physiology.

The entire chapter on the teaching of the natural law in matters which pertain to the morality of artificial contraception is oversimplified. In his defense of the "natural," and to his mind, "lawful" use of the progestational steroids as contraceptive devices, Dr. Rock does not meet the incisive arguments against his position which have been continually voiced by Catholic moral theologians.

In the pages of this book, Dr. Rock is emphatic in his claim to be a good and devoted Catholic. It must be said, however, that some of the positions which he defends therein are not in agreement with Catholic teachers.

Theologians must recognize the competence of Dr. Rock in the field of reproductive physiology, but he must recognize their competence in the field of Catholic moral teaching.

The book sold, and Dr. Rock continued to practice his faith as a Catholic. And there were indications that, all in all, the prelate's comments were a gentle birching from which the physician recovered without complications.

Further indication that the Church was taking a more relaxed view of the issue came a little more than a year later when Dr. Joseph L. Dorsey, also a Catholic, in an article in the *New England Journal of Medicine,* urged repeal of the Massachusetts law. And in a foreword, Monsignor Lally commented that "most people in the community, in my judgment, feel with him that the time is ripe for reconsidering the question in the light of the claims of a plural society."

Dr. Dorsey said that repeal would eliminate hard feelings between Catholics and non-Catholics, asserting that the existing law was "an albatross around the neck of Catholics whenever religious liberty is brought up." He suggested that neither the Catholic Church nor the Protestant-dominated Planned Parenthood League should lead the repeal movement but rather it should be spearheaded by a group of citizens of all faiths.

On his return from the third session of the Ecumenical Council, Cardinal Cushing made his most outspoken statement to date on the subject of birth control. As cardinal, Cushing has not merely followed the new liberalism of the Church; his influence at the Council has made it evident that he is one of its leading spirits. He seems to feel a new freedom to say what he had thought before the Council convened.

Speaking at a communion breakfast at which he had accepted a check for $10,000 from representatives of the fishing and waterfront industries, Cardinal Cushing said that the Church had a staff of medical experts studying the problem of birth control.

Looking out over his glasses he commented, "We are hopeful of coming up with a foolproof natural birth control method or else we will have to pass new laws at the next Ecumenical Council."

His comment was far from the traditional stand of the Church on the subject—which allowed of no change or exceptions—and it carried the authority of one of the foremost members of the Sacred College of Cardinals.

CHAPTER XIV

Death of a Pope

Two events in 1963 brought grief to the entire free world, plunged the Boston community into mourning, and were a particularly poignant sorrow to Richard Cardinal Cushing. One was the death on June 3 of Pope John XXIII; the other was the assassination on November 22 of President John F. Kennedy. With Pope John, Cushing had a deep spiritual affinity; during his reign he had risen to new heights as a prelate and had found a broader scope for his energies and his ideas. To John F. Kennedy, a native Bostonian, and the first Catholic President, Cushing had been spiritual adviser and a close personal friend. On both occasions the duties of his office and his personal burden of sorrow were heavy.

Cardinal Cushing was notified of the Pontiff's death by Monsignor Lally, editor of the *Pilot*. The prelate immediately issued a statement asserting, "Today the whole human family is desolate—we have lost our common father."

The Pope's character, said Cardinal Cushing, had "surmounted every barrier, dissolved the most ancient prejudices and captured not merely the imagination, but the hearts of men everywhere.

"Pope John was the best human reproduction of Christ that I have ever met."

Cardinal Cushing made immediate plans to fly to Rome on Sunday for the election of a new Pope. On Thursday, an archdiocesan day of official mourning, he celebrated a televised mass at Holy Cross Cathedral. Within the Gothic edifice lay a draped catafalque, representing a coffin. It rested there through the traditional nine-day period of mourning.

Nearly 4,000 persons, chiefly priests and nuns, crowded the Cathedral, and another 1,500 persons followed the ceremony in the lower church over television. Outside, the sidewalks were packed with hundreds more. The Elevated trains slowed to a crawl passing the cathedral, to keep down the noise.

Cardinal Cushing, clad in black vestments with a white miter, hailed the dead Pope as the "builder of bridges" between Catholics and Protestants, between East and West and between Christians and non-Christians.

"He lifted the Catholic Church from its moorings of past ages into the bewildering chaos of the twentieth century," said Cardinal Cushing. "His goodness will live forever."

At the close of the mass, Cardinal Cushing embraced with the "kiss of peace" Bishop Frederic C. Lawrence, suffragan of the Episcopal diocese, and Bishop Gerasimo of the Greek Orthodox Church, who were seated in the sanctuary.

Although he had been forced to rearrange his schedule because of the trip to Rome, the Cardinal went ahead with a scheduled appearance at the first graduating exercises at

St. Peter's High School in Cambridge. He called on the 33 seniors to follow the example of "Good Pope John."

The effect of the Pope's death on the entire Boston community would have been unimaginable fifty years before; the response of people of all faiths was a testimony of the goodwill that existed among various denominations, partly due to Cardinal Cushing's years of effort toward establishing warm relations between Catholics and non-Catholics and partly due to the outgoing character of Pope John. When the news of his death was received, Dean Charles H. Buck, Jr., of the Episcopal Cathedral Church of St. Paul ordered his edifice to be draped in black—the first time this had ever been done in honor of the head of another denomination. On the following Sunday evening, June 9, Bishop Anson Phelps Stokes, Jr., presided at an interfaith memorial service there, with the clergy of ten faiths participating.

By this time Cardinal Cushing was already en route to Rome to take part in the election of a new Pope. He was represented at St. Paul's Cathedral by Monsignor Murray, attired in the red robes of his rank, who walked in the processional and knelt at a prie-dieu in the chancel. Opposite him was seated Rabbi Saul Gurvitz.

Portions of the service were shared by Bishop Stokes, Bishop James K. Mathews of the Methodist Church, Dr. Paul L. Sturges of the Massachusetts Baptist Convention, Dr. Albert J. Penner of the Massachusetts Congregational Christian Conference, and the Rev. Dr. Forrest L. Knapp of the Massachusetts Council of Churches. Nine Protestant denominations were represented.

Prof. George H. Williams of the Harvard Divinity School preached the sermon. A Protestant observer at the first session of the Ecumenical Council in Rome, Professor

Williams said that Pope John "liberated the Catholic Church from a kind of captivity within the framework of West European society and moved all Christians to shed the captive fetters of a too parochial, or a too nationalistic, or a too classbound, or a too time-bound version of the faith."

At the airport that evening, a crowd of close to 1,000 had wished the Cardinal godspeed. It would be the second time that a Boston prelate participated in the election of a Pope. Cardinal O'Connell had taken part in only one of the three elections for which he was eligible during his reign. In those days, church law provided that balloting for a new Pope should begin nine days after the death of the Pontiff. Restricted to steamship travel across the Atlantic, Cardinal O'Connell arrived 24 hours too late in 1914 and only two hours too late in 1922. With typical O'Connell indignation, the old Bostonian argued and won the point that longer travel time should be allowed to accommodate non-Italian cardinals. Pope Pius XI had the law changed. And when that Pontiff died in 1939, Cardinal O'Connell was on hand in plenty of time for the election of Pope Pius XII.

Even though he had time to spare, Cardinal Cushing's plane was delayed nearly an hour when some cargo had to be removed to comply with runway weight restrictions.

"I would rather stay, but I got a telegram today telling me to hurry up," commented Cardinal Cushing as he boarded the jet liner with Monsignor Robert J. Sennott, chancellor of the archdiocese.

When the Cardinal arrived in Rome the following day, he was welcomed by a group which included Monsignor Daniel Cronin, a native of Cambridge, Massachusetts, who had been selected to be the Bostonian's one permitted attendant after he entered the Sistine Chapel for the balloting on June 19. Monsignor Cronin had been attached to the Vatican secretariat for two years.

By now a familiar figure known for his cooperation with quotable snap comments, Cardinal Cushing was sought out by newspaper and electronic reporters alike. He assured them that the new Pope would carry on the work started by John.

He was asked to comment on a speculative story in a Milan newspaper that he might be considered "papabile," or a possibility for Pope.

"I'm afraid not," replied the Bostonian with a guffaw. "If I were ever elected Pope that would be the end of the apostolic succession. All I want to do is help people."

Cardinal Cushing was housed during the early part of his stay at the villa of the North American College 22 miles outside of Rome. Each day, he took part in the sessions of the College of Cardinals, who served as an interregnum committee to handle affairs of the Church during the hiatus between Popes.

"I don't think a non-Italian will be elected," Cardinal Cushing told the Boston reporters who accompanied him on the trip. "He has to be head of the Vatican state. In listening to predictions, remember, there is a saying that is very popular—that is: 'The man who goes into the election a Pope, comes out a cardinal.' "

The body of Pope John was laid to rest temporarily in the grottoes beneath the huge Basilica of St. Peter's on June 6. Until a few hours before his burial, a steady river of mourners, 15 to 20 abreast, surged through St. Peter's Square into the church to pay their last respects. An estimated 1,000,000 persons passed the bier before the doors were closed the final day.

Then, for the benefit of nearly 300,000 still waiting in

"I've got a voice like a fish peddler." The Cardinal singing at a party at Blinstrub's.

Boston. Mrs. Edward M. Kennedy looks on as Richard Cardinal Cushing of Boston welcomes the audience to a fashion show of Oleg Cassini designs held in the Statler Hilton Hotel in Boston for the benefit of the Richard Cardinal Cushing Charity Fund. *Courtesy Wide World Photos*

Bishop Anson Phelps Stokes, Jr., Episcopal diocese of Massachusetts, at Trinity Church luncheon with Cardinal Cushing. *Courtesy the Boston Herald*

Cardinal Cushing kneeling in meditation in Trinity Church, Boston, with the Rev. Dr. Theodore P. Ferris, rector of Trinity. *Courtesy the Boston Herald*

Cardinal Cushing with President John F. Kennedy. *Courtesy the Boston Herald*

Cardinal Cushing in Rome, center, with Monsignor George A. Schlicte, new rector of Pope John XIII Seminary, left, and Monsignor Robert J. Sennot of Boston. *Courtesy The Pilot*

Cardinal Richard J. Cushing elevating chalice during Mass. *Courtesy The Pilot*

Good old New England humor. President John F. Kennedy laughs as he chats with Richard Cardinal Cushing, Archbishop of Boston, Kennedy's home territory, during the chief executive's visit to the Pontifical North American College in Rome.

Archbishop Richard Cardinal Cushing conducts a funeral Mass over the flag-covered casket of John F. Kennedy in St. Matthew's Roman Catholic Cathedral, Washington, on November 24, 1963.

Archbishop Richard Cardinal Cushing of Boston greets the widow of President Kennedy as she arrives at St. Matthew's Roman Catholic Cathedral in Washington, November 24, 1963.

line the bier was carried out onto the porch of the Basilica
and tilted so the crowd could get a better view of the red-
clad body of the eighty-one-year-old Pontiff. A sudden hush
fell. Many people crossed themselves, but most of them just
stared. After nearly a quarter of an hour, the body was
taken back inside and encased in a triple coffin of cypress,
lead and elm.

As the throngs were paying their final respects and cardinals were streaming in from all corners of the globe, the
Pope's last will and testament had been disclosed. It said
that he awaited death "simply and happily," and asked that
his body be buried finally beneath the Basilica of St. John
Lateran. His few worldly goods were left to three surviving
brothers and a sister.

The Pope personally had ordered one change in the in-
terment procedure. Instead of the papal coffin's being low-
ered into the grottoes by a winch through a hole in the
floor of the basilica, he had said that it should be carried to
the grottoes through a side entrance.

Otherwise, ritual proceeded according to ancient practices. This included daily masses for nine days. Before the
coffin was sealed, a purse containing medals and coins
minted during the Pope's reign was placed at his feet. The
coffin was placed beneath St. Peter's for the time being since
the tomb in St. John's, named after Saints John the Baptist
and John the Evangelist, was not immediately ready to receive it.

During the wait between the final obsequies and the balloting, Cardinal Cushing learned that the United States Supreme Court had banned the reading of the Bible and the
reciting of the Lord's Prayer in public schools. He immediately branded it "a victory for Communism," and urged an
amendment to the Constitution of offset the decision.

"To me, it is a great tragedy that the greatest book that was ever published and the best seller of the ages cannot be read in our public school system of education," he said.

The Sistine Chapel cell to which Cardinal Cushing was assigned for the balloting was an accountant's office converted into simple living quarters for the conclave. The eighty Princes of the Church on hand for the occasion were locked in the chapel for the duration of deliberations, along with 200 assistants and Vatican personnel. They also were sworn to secrecy about the conclave.

The ballots were burned in a small cast-iron stove after each vote. The ballots were mixed with damp straw after an unsuccessful vote, creating black smoke. Dry straw created white smoke, the sign that a new Pope had been elected.

Two days and five ballots after they began deliberating, the eighty cardinals chose Batista Cardinal Montini, Archbishop of Milan. He took the name Paul VI. Unlike his peasant predecessor, Pope Paul was the son of a prosperous lawyer and journalist. He had been a member of the Vatican secretariat since 1922. He was sixty-five, a relative stripling in the hierarchy, and was one of the 23 cardinals created by John in 1958.

Cardinal Cushing's reaction was that "he was the very best choice that could be made.

"I am confident we have what I wanted, a mission-minded Pope, a Pope who has visited the United States and has a great admiration for the Catholics of our country," said the Cardinal.

"He speaks English well enough," the Bostonian went on. "He stayed with me at Lake Street for two days the last time he was in the country and he gave a Latin address to the seminarians at St. John's."

The Boston cardinal said that there had been some opposition to Cardinal Montini, but that "it was very weak."
He disclosed that there had been some votes for him, but
he declined to say how many. On returning to his quarters
at the North American College, Cardinal Cushing jokingly
said, "Well, I didn't make it."

"But did you see the size of that crowd?" he added, moving his head in the direction of St. Peter's Square where
throngs were gathering to wait for a glimpse of the new
Pontiff.

The following day, the Cardinal expressed anxiety over
losing donations needed to support his vast charities and
building program back in Boston.

"Let's say I'm concerned," he told those around him,
"not worried, but positively concerned. I have to collect $8,-
000,000 a year to keep the special works of the Boston Archdiocese and our Latin American programs running the way
they should.

"When I'm home, I can raise it. But I've learned, on previous trips out of the country, that our charity alms are
reduced to a very low level when I go away. As a matter of
fact, they drop off about $16,000 a day."

Finally, on June 25, Cardinal Cushing said, "We are
going home to Boston on Monday. I would have gone earlier but the President of the United States is coming to
Rome. He won't be here for the coronation of Pope Paul,
but he may want to see me.

"I hope he wants to see me," the prelate added with a
wink, "because if I stay in Rome any longer I'll be in the
poorhouse."

The Cardinal remained on to see President Kennedy and
to join him in an audience with the new Pope. When the
President arrived at the North American College with his

sister, Mrs. Stephen Smith, Cardinal Cushing kissed her on both cheeks and exclaimed, "Hi, Jean! My, you look good!"

Then he turned his attention to the President. First he shook hands with Mr. Kennedy, then he poked him in the chest and put up his fists in an exaggerated ring pose. The President looked startled for a moment, then he broke into laughter, joined by the Cardinal.

Almost immediately, with his facility for switching moods, the Cardinal became serious. He gave Mr. Kennedy some gifts Pope John had intended to present to him. They included one of only three autographed copies of the late Pope's encyclical, "Pacem in Terris," and two sets of silver, bronze and gold medallions commemorating another encyclical, "Mater et Magistra."

Later, after the President's audience with Pope Paul, the Cardinal described it as a "magnificent tribute of affection and esteem by the Holy Father to the President and the citizens of the United States." Cardinal Cushing said the Pope gave Mr. Kennedy a solid gold rosary for his wife, Jacqueline, and three gold medals for his children, the impending arrival of the third having kept her at home.

The coronation of the 262nd Supreme Pontiff of the Roman Church on June 30, on the Feast of St. Paul, was attended by a throng estimated at 250,000. For the first time in the twentieth century, the two-and-a-half-hour ceremony took place on the porch of St. Peter's. The triple crown, a modern lightweight headpiece, was placed on the head of Paul VI by Alfredo Cardinal Ottaviani, Secretary of the Sacred Supreme Congregation.

He intoned: "Receive this tiara, adorned with three crowns, and know that you are the father of princes and kings, guide of the world and vicar of Christ Jesus our Saviour."

The new Pope of a billion and a half Catholics spoke in nine languages, including Latin, English and Russian, asserting that neither peace nor unity was easily come by. He pleaded for "greater mutual comprehension, charity and peace between peoples."

Three times, the Pope was borne around St. Peter's Square on a portable throne and thrice a functionary burned a piece of flax before his eyes, intoning, *"Pater sancte sic transit gloria mundi*—Holy Father, thus passes the glory of the world."

During part of the ceremony, the Pope celebrated mass, receiving at the close a white silk purse with 25 coins in payment for "a mass well sung," and symbolizing that he, too, was a priest.

The Boston cardinal arrived back home on July 2, 1963. He told reporters he had received one of two papal crosses used by Pope John, asserting, "I got the better one." But he said he was "not at liberty" to disclose who got the other.

Describing his stay as "very tiresome and arduous," the Cardinal said that instead of taking a vacation, "I am going to stay home and collect money.

"As a matter of fact," he said with a sly grin, "I'd like to take up a collection, now, but I'll put that off until later."

CHAPTER XV

Cardinal Cushing and the Kennedy Family

DURING the period when Richard James Cushing was wrestling with his conscience at the crossroads between the priesthood and politics in South Boston, Joseph Patrick Kennedy was preparing to emigrate from East Boston, across the harbor, on a pilgrimage that was to bring him fortune, position, power and an overflowing cup of personal triumph and tragedy.

Although Kennedy was the elder by seven years, the two men were much alike, as products of the mores of that era. Despite a Harvard education and a budding genius for high finance, Kennedy found himself, as an Irishman, repeatedly frozen out by the codfish Yankees. He finally declared himself.

"I was born here, my children were born here; what the hell do I have to do to be called an American?" he snapped one day. He soon decided the best thing to do was to get out of such a stultifying atmosphere. Shifting his sights, Kennedy took his wife and growing family to New York, and transferred his business interests to Chicago, Hollywood and elsewhere. He soon was moving into the million-aire class.

Joseph Kennedy had one major asset as a counterweight to his personal aggressiveness. He had married Rose Fitz-gerald. To Cardinal Cushing, she is "a saint." She was the daughter of John F. Fitzgerald, another fighting Irishman who had chosen the field of Boston politics. Fitzgerald and Pat Kennedy, Joe's father, were allies in the struggle for rec-ognition, the former as an officeholder and the latter as a kingmaker behind the scenes.

Rose Kennedy bore Joseph nine children, four boys and five girls. And the family kept a tie to Massachusetts by establishing a summer home at Hyannis Port, on Cape Cod. In later years, when it fell to the lot of the second son, John Fitzgerald Kennedy, to launch a political career in Massachusetts, the family had acquired a detached air of amusement toward the pretensions of those who sought places on the bandwagon.

Richard Cushing, who remained in Boston after choos-ing the road to the priesthood, had his say about the early frustrations of the Irish long after the Kennedys had made their mark elsewhere. And he repeated it occasionally, ap-parently when the black mood was upon him. At a com-munion breakfast of State House employees in the spring of 1964, Cardinal Cushing commented, after receiving a check for his charity fund, "I am a poor man myself; if I had wanted to be rich, I would have become a politician.

"Forty years ago, the only places for an Irishman in Bos-ton were in the Church or in politics; as far as banking was concerned, 'Irish need not apply.' "

Yet it was as a financier that Joseph Kennedy had made a fortune even before he left Boston. But the bitterness of many Irish Catholics over their condition remained, even though, after World War II, the social climate of Boston was far less murky than it had been in previous years.

World War II was over by the time the paths of the expatriate Joseph Kennedy and the missionary-minded but homebound South Boston priest, Richard Cushing, finally crossed. Kennedy had attained position as Ambassador to Great Britain and wealth through a series of financial coups. But he also had drunk deeply of the cup of bitterness. One son, Lieut. Joseph P. Kennedy, Jr., had died a hero's death as a naval flier in a crash over the English Channel. Another, Lieut. (j.g.) John F. Kennedy, had been seriously wounded in heroic action as commander of PT-Boat 109, in the Pacific. One daughter, Kathleen, the Marchioness of Huntington, had died in a civilian air crash in Britain, her new home. Another, Rosemary, a retarded child from birth, was in an institution.

Richard Cushing, on the other hand, had gained his information about global affairs from the lips of missionary priests through his work as director of the Society for the Propagation of the Faith. And he had become Archbishop of Boston. One of his first associations with Joseph Kennedy, he recalled, was when the former ambassador asked him to arrange for a special cottage to be built for Rosemary at St. Coletta's. Kennedy offered to foot the bill.

"But I told him that most of our land down there was wooded, and if we built a separate building, people would immediately ask, 'Who lives there?' " said the Cardinal, recently, in an informal interview at his residence.

"So, he asked me where she could be placed, under similar good care, and I told him of another St. Coletta's out in Jefferson, Wisconsin, and he agreed to that," the Cardinal said.

"You know," he commented in an aside, "the reason I have always said that I want to be buried in Hanover, at our St. Coletta's, right there among all those kids, is that they are the ones who will really pray for you.

"Cardinal O'Connell has a tomb right here on the place, but I have never seen anyone out praying for him," he chuckled.

"At first, Joe and I didn't hit it off at all," the Cardinal went on, "but finally Bart Brickley, who was his lawyer, said to me, 'The trouble with you two is you are like two peas in a pod; why don't you call him up?'

"I said I wouldn't call him up because I didn't want anything from him," said the Cardinal, "but we got along well enough later. Actually, I had nothing to do with the Kennedys socially; they came from a different background from mine. My father was a blacksmith. I have spent most of my time with little people, trying to help them. But the Kennedys have been good to me, as their spiritual adviser, and, of course, I have been good to them."

Individually, as the result of their wanderings, the Kennedys had no firm parish roots until Hyannis Port more and more became a focal point for periodic reunions. There, in nearby Hyannis, they became regular communicants at St. Francis Xavier and gave generously to the parish, donating an altar in memory of Joe, Jr. And the most faithful attendant at mass was Rose Kennedy, from whom they inherited a deep sense of religious obligation.

Later, as the Kennedys apparently overcame their reticence about Rosemary, the family foundation began making grants for research and for facilities. A hospital for handicapped children, named in memory of Joseph, Jr., was erected in Boston by the Cardinal, with the help of foundation funds. But the bulk of the money was raised by the prelate himself.

"Joe always wanted to know where the money was going; he never wasted money or time," the Cardinal said in a reminiscent mood. "If he arranged to give you an hour at the Cape, you would probably go out on the boat and have some chowder and a boiled lobster for lunch, but as soon as the business was finished and the hour was up, he ordered the boat turned back for the dock.

"But I'll say this for Joe," the Cardinal went on. "He once told me, 'People think I am interested only in making money; my main interest is the success of my children.'"

Possibly, seeing in Jack Kennedy the political image of what he might have been had he not chosen the Church, Cardinal Cushing, then still Archbishop, took an interest in the scrawny young man when he became a candidate for Congress from the Eleventh Massachusetts District in 1946.

"Jack was terribly shy and had trouble making speeches," the Cardinal recalled, "so I told his campaign managers to stress the idea of question and answer presentations, and you remember how effective he became eventually in press conferences and, of course, in the debates with Nixon."

Six years later, after having served three terms in Congress, John F. Kennedy took Massachusetts by storm, with the help of his mother and sisters at a hundred tea party receptions around the commonwealth, and was elected to the Senate. It was a Republican year that saw General of the Army Dwight D. Eisenhower elected President. But Yankee Republican Henry Cabot Lodge was no match for the rising young Democrat, Kennedy, and was spilled out of his Senate seat into an ocean of tea.

The Kennedy victory was the first in a series of reversals

for the Lodges over a period of years in Massachusetts. Back in 1916, Senator Lodge's grandfather, the first Henry Cabot Lodge, had turned back a bid for the same Senate seat by John F. Fitzgerald.

Young Senator Kennedy, in 1953, scored another triumph. He won the hand of Miss Jacqueline Lee Bouvier of Washington and Newport, Rhode Island. He met her when she was doing an inquiring photographer column for the Washington *Times-Herald*. Miss Bouvier, the daughter of Mrs. Hugh D. Auchincloss, had been brought up in international society. When the young couple decided to be married in century-old St. Mary's Church, in Newport, they asked Archbishop Cushing of Boston to officiate.

The 11 A.M. nuptial mass on September 12, 1953, was attended by an impressive gathering of society and politics. Robert F. Kennedy was his brother's best man. The fourteen ushers included such names as Charles L. Bartlett, a Washington newspaperman; Senator George Smathers of Florida; R. Sargent Shriver of Chicago; Benjamin Smith 2d, of Gloucester, Massachusetts, and Edward M. Kennedy of Hyannis Port.

Mrs. Michael T. Canfield of New York City was her sister's matron of honor. And the bridesmaids included Miss Jean Kennedy of Palm Beach, Florida, Miss Nancy Tuckerman of New York City and Miss Shirley Oakes of London. James Lee Auchincloss of Newport, the page, was noted by one reporter to be having trouble with a loose front tooth.

Another reporter commented the next morning in his story, "Only on such an occasion would you see confirmed New Dealers like Dean Jim Landis and Rep. Tom Dodd of Hartford fraternizing with hard-shelled Republicans like Speaker Joe Martin and Senator Leverett Saltonstall."

Although denied the Democratic nomination for Vice-

President in 1956, Senator Kennedy won re-election to his own seat so handily in November that year that his stock as a favorite son for 1960 began to rise. It was given one boost before a highly receptive communion breakfast audience of 1,500 telephone company workers by the Archbishop of Boston. The Senator spoke first on foreign policy, asserting that the crushing of the Hungarian revolt had switched the balance of power to the West because it had shown "the uncommitted nations, such as India, the true nature of Communism."

The Archbishop followed this up by telling his audience that Senator Kennedy was a young man who, "if it pleases God, we shall follow to the most exalted heights that are within the power of the people of the United States to give him.

"The hope of this country lies in the elected officials of the caliber of Senator Kennedy," said the prelate. "Youthful in appearance, mature on every level, of tremendous potential power, he has the courage, the great hope of the future; not yet on the heights, but still climbing."

As his father had before him, in pursuing a career in finance, so John F. Kennedy, in politics, lived a nomadic life away from home much of the time. But the Cardinal remembered the young politician occasionally dropping by to leave a check.

"And if it was at a time when I was broadcasting the Rosary," said the prelate, "he would kneel in the chapel and tell the beads."

The two years remaining before the 1960 election stirred up old national religious animosities that had been more or less dormant since the unsuccessful Presidential bid of New York's Al Smith, in 1928.

Addressing dedication ceremonies at the Joseph P. Kennedy, Jr., School in Hyde Park, Massachusetts, September 23, 1957, Cardinal Cushing asserted that he became upset "when I hear that a Catholic cannot become President of the United States; one's church has nothing to do with it." He said that he considered Senator Kennedy well equipped for the Presidency, but cautiously added, "as are others.

"I don't believe a Catholic should vote for a Catholic, just because he is a Catholic," said the Cardinal. "I believe people of all faiths think the same, that religion has nothing to do with a man's holding public office, the highest or the lowest."

The Cardinal's feelings were not always shared by all of his flock. For during the same period, a prominent Boston Irish politician, talking confidentially with a political reporter, said, "When I go in that booth, I'm a Catholic first and a Democrat second."

Senator Kennedy was on hand in Boston for the sesquicentennial dinner of the archdiocese, May 11, 1958. By then, he not only was being seriously considered as a candidate for the Presidency, but also he was beginning to face the slings and arrows of those intent on injecting religion into the situation.

Cardinal Cushing asserted, "I have never met any ecclesiastical leader who desired the union of the state and church in this country, and I, for one, want absolutely no part of anything of the kind."

In his speech, the young Senator noted that the establishment of the archdiocese in 1808 had not even been mentioned in the newspapers.

"Now, in an age when disintegration is our constant companion, it is good to be a part of an institution which has shown its ability to survive," he said. And in a tribute to the Cardinal, Senator Kennedy predicted that "his example of devotion and faith will remain long after his buildings have crumbled away."

Just about a year later, the Senator stirred up a rumpus among some Catholics by an interview published by *Look* magazine. The Senator told the interviewer that he opposed the appointment of a United States ambassador to the Vatican and that he opposed Federal aid to any religious school. Moreover, he asserted that "whatever one's religion in private life may be, for the officeholder nothing takes precedence over his oath to uphold the Constitution and all its parts, including the First Amendment and the strict separation of church and state."

Later, in a speech to the Lantern Club of Boston, a group of advertising representatives of national magazines, Cardinal Cushing asserted, "I think it is a great pity that questions of this sort still have to be answered at all.

"They are certainly ridiculous when presented to a person who has been in public life as long as Senator Kennedy," he went on. "The patriotic qualities of the Senator were written in dramatic and dangerous actions during the war; they were challenged by enemy conflict and finally honored by citation.

"They also have been tested in peace and the record lies open in Congress before the nation. His life and record are the best commentaries on his convictions and from my personal knowledge of him I can say without hesitation that Senator Kennedy will always perform his public duties to the highest standards of conscience and his oath of office."

The attacks by several Catholic publications outside of Massachusetts were so sharp that Methodist Bishop John Wesley Lord of Boston told delegates to a New England

Methodist Conference that the criticism surely had embarrassed and surprised the Senator.

The bishop also expressed praise for Cardinal Cushing's support of young Kennedy. Noting that the Senator had said that nothing would take precedence over his oath of office, Bishop Lord added, "If a man is willing to do this, I do not see how his conscience in other matters can be called into question."

From time to time through the election year of 1960, Cardinal Cushing was moved to defend Senator Kennedy from snide references to clerical dictation. He also asserted, in June, before the convention, that he was not politically endorsing any candidate.

"Senator Kennedy would resent absolutely having a cardinal, a bishop or a priest telling him how to act," said the prelate. "I don't know anyone who would try to tell him. I hope and pray that once and for all we'll be able to eliminate the religious issue from politics."

Several times, the Cardinal insisted there was no such thing as a Catholic vote.

"As far as I can make out," he said once, "the only thing Catholics agree on is the dogma mentioned in the Apostle's Creed."

A few days before the election, the Cardinal was in Las Vegas, Nevada, to address a convention of the National Council of Catholic Women. He branded as a "colossal lie" a charge in a newspaper editorial that he had once influenced Senator Kennedy to change his vote on Federal aid to education.

The charge was attributed to Dr. Willard Givens, director of education of the Supreme Council of Scottish Rite Masons, Southern District. Dr. Givens said later that he had discussed the matter with Kennedy ten years before.

Cardinal Cushing said that he had been represented as warning Kennedy that if he wanted to keep his seat in Congress he would have to vote against the aid bill.

"I deny the entire matter," the Cardinal said. "I deny every reference to me in that editorial. Never have I telephoned Mr. Kennedy in Congress, at his home or anywhere else. Never have I requested him or any other person to change their vote on any matter."

And the Cardinal urged the Catholic women to "vote for whom you wish. You vote in accordance with your conscience. Never vote for anyone because he or she is of a specific faith, nationality or color."

Despite his personal interest in the young Senator, Cardinal Cushing said later, "The brains behind the campaign was Joe. Hour after hour, he was on the telephone, calling people all over the country.

"You know," he continued, "Joe had a falling out with Spellman, because the Cardinal attended a dinner where Nixon and Eisenhower were present and he thought that meant he was supporting them.

"Joe called me about a list of bishops he had who hadn't come out in support of Jack," the Cardinal recalled, "and I told him, 'Mr. Ambassador, the fact that they do not take part in a political campaign is not a sign they are against him,' but I'm not sure Joe was convinced.

"I had hoped that Jack would win by a plurality of three or four million, but, of course, it was very close," said the Cardinal, "and, as a matter of fact, he would have had a hard time winning a second term.

"First of all, Cuba would have been an Achilles' heel, and then he had a far vaster plan for combating poverty than Johnson put across, and big business knew it and was out to get him.

"But Jack was completely dedicated to his job," his spiritual adviser said. "He had two major goals: first, no war, because no one could win and the real losers would be the little people; and second, he was anxious to create a lasting image as the first Catholic President."

With the election at last over, President-elect Kennedy, in making plans for his inauguration, invited his spiritual director to deliver the invocation. The Cardinal's trip to Washington became the basis for one of his classic stories. He first told it to a group of 200 attendants at the National Catholic Camping Association convention in Boston, a week later.

Cardinal Cushing said that he had made arrangements, first of all, to stay in Washington with Bishop Patrick A. O'Boyle, "because I think one of the things it takes to become an old soldier is to stay away from the big guns," a Cushingism that he used frequently.

But the plane carrying him to the capital circled Washington for more than an hour, because of snow, then was unable to get in to Philadelphia and finally turned back to Idlewild Airport in New York.

The prelate took a bus from the airport to Pennsylvania Station, arriving there at 1 A.M. on January 19, Inauguration Day.

"There were no redcaps, and I spent more than an hour sitting on my suitcase waiting for a train, because of the strike," the Cardinal related. "In an attempt to get warm, I ordered some oyster stew and even that did not have any oysters in it."

When he finally reached Washington, by day coach, at 5:45 A.M., Bishop O'Boyle was waiting for him. They went to the rectory for coffee. He continued:

"Now, you get the worst coffee in the world in convents, and the second worst in rectories, but Bishop O'Boyle makes one of the best cups of coffee I ever had. He has the magic touch.

"He told me that I would not be able to get any sleep because I was scheduled to say mass at the national shrine. The mass was well attended in spite of the storm.

"I went from there to the Inauguration ceremonies, and I have never been so cold in my life.

"When I got to the Inauguration, the crowd was assembled, and I was sitting next to a protocol officer of the State Department.

"Just before I got up to give the invocation, I said to him, 'There's a fire in that lectern, can't you see the smoke?'

"He said, 'That's just steam.'

"And I said, 'Well, I guess it's being made by the hot air from all these politicians.'

"As I went up to start the invocation, the thought crossed my mind there might be a bomb in the lectern, and I thought, if there was, I would probably land somewhere over near the Washington Monument.

"But I figured it would probably get me first, and might save the lives of a few other people. But I hoped it wouldn't go off.

"While I was talking, there was a fireman with a fire extinguisher at my back. I decided that if the extinguisher went off the spray would turn me into one big icicle. I've heard of a lot of people being under fire but this was the first time I found myself with a group of people over a fire. I finished my little assignment and that was all I saw of the Inauguration."

A national television audience would remember the Inauguration for the Cardinal's calm delivery of perhaps one of the longest invocations on record, as well as for the difficulty Robert Frost, the poet, had in reading a work he had written for the occasion, because of the chill wind.

Later in the year, Joseph Kennedy suffered a stroke while playing golf with his niece, Ann Gargan, at the West Palm Beach Country Club. Cardinal Cushing, who had gone to Peru to attend the funeral of an Irish missionary priest, arranged to stop off to see the elder Kennedy in the hospital.

The Boston prelate found the family patriarch asleep, and after saying some prayers and a blessing, went outside to talk with Robert and Edward Kennedy. The second time he visited the room Kennedy was awake.

Again the Cardinal blessed him, and said, "Keep up your courage, Joe, you'll make it."

Later, in recalling the Florida stopover, Cardinal Cushing has told visitors, "He didn't look well at all, but you can't discount this man's courage."

Although Cardinal Cushing had married the President and Jacqueline Bouvier and baptized their children, it was not until July 19, 1963, that he performed a similar service for one of the other Kennedys. This was the baptism of Christopher George Kennedy, eighth child of Attorney General and Mrs. Robert Kennedy. The President and his daughter, Caroline, were on hand with thirty Kennedys and guests in the crowded sacristy of St. Francis Xavier's in Hyannis. After the ceremony, the Cardinal looked down at Christopher and said, "If you don't become a priest, a bishop or a cardinal, it won't be my fault."

Jacqueline Kennedy, expecting another child soon, was not at the baptism. Then, a few weeks later, on August 9, her second son, Patrick Bouvier Kennedy, died at the Children's Medical Center in Boston less than forty hours after his birth.

The infant, suffering from respiratory deficiency, had been born at the Otis Air Force Base Hospital, near Hyannis, August 7. Father John Scahill, the Base Catholic chaplain, baptized the child when it was apparent he was in serious condition. Despite a team of physicians summoned to treat the youngster, after he had been rushed over the road to Boston, he failed to respond.

Cardinal Cushing celebrated the Mass of the Angels for little Patrick in his private chapel on August 10. The grief-stricken President sat alone in the right-hand front pew. He and his entourage, including members of the family, arrived in four helicopters from Otis, landing on a baseball field on the grounds of St. John's Seminary, nearby. Cardinal Spellman knelt on a prie-dieu in the rear of the chapel.

The low mass was completed in twenty-five minutes. The body of the infant rested in a gold and white coffin in front of the altar rail. A blanket of white carnations was draped over it. The altar was decorated with white carnations, gladioli and snapdragons.

Later, the coffin was borne to Holyhood Cemetery in suburban Brookline to be buried in a family plot purchased fifteen years before by Joseph P. Kennedy.

Recalling the occasion some months later, Cardinal Cushing said, "I will never forget the day that we buried the little child, Patrick Bouvier Kennedy. Jack was the last to leave the chapel. I followed him. The little casket containing the body was at the head of the aisle. Jack put his arms around the casket as if he wanted to carry it with him. Then, the tears watered his cheeks."

At the cemetery, after the committal prayers, the President walked over to the coffin, rested his hand on it for a few moments and then turned and walked back to his car.

Two months later, only a short time before his own death, the President, on a visit to Harvard to select a site for a library for his state papers, managed to break away from the public spotlight to visit the grave of little Patrick. He stood silently for several moments before turning away and resuming his official duties. Afterward, other visitors found a small bouquet of yellow chrysanthemums on the grave.

The Kennedy plot is on a gentle knoll in Holyhood. It is marked by a white granite monument seven feet long and four feet high. The name Kennedy is marked in bas-relief, flanked by two representations of pilasters, with modified Corinthian capitals. On either side of the pilasters is a panel with a representation of a spray of flowers. And on either end of the monument is a Latin cross, also in bas-relief. Evergreen shrubs and a double row of hemlocks soften the severe starkness of the stone.

An assassination, in Dallas, Texas, on November 22, 1963, changed many things—even the final resting place of a child that lived only a few hours. The body of Patrick Bouvier Kennedy subsequently was removed from Holyhood to be buried with that of his father, John F. Kennedy, in the Arlington Memorial Cemetery in Washington.

News that an assassin's bullet had struck down President Kennedy as he rode beside his wife in an open car in Dallas on that November afternoon sped around the world like an electric shock. In Boston, Cardinal Cushing retired to his private chapel, weeping unashamedly, to pray.

The following day he said, "My heart is broken with grief over his martyrdom for the cause of the free world. My prayers go forth in sympathy to his dear wife, and all members of his family. John F. Kennedy, known to me for a lifetime, loved by me as a devoted friend, has laid down his life for all men. Greater love than this no man has."

Most of the Kennedy family gathered at Hyannis Port, within a few hours after the assassination. Although unable through the press of duties to go to Cape Cod immediately, Cardinal Cushing was asked to preside at the funeral mass for the President in Washington, on November 25.

The day before, in a nationally telecast ceremony, the Cardinal celebrated a memorial mass at the Boston archdiocesan television center. At the close of the mass, Cardinal Cushing turned to the cameras to pay tribute to a young husband and father whom the nation had known as Mr. President.

"I have been with him in joy and in sorrow, in decision and in crisis, among friends and with strangers, and I know of no one who has combined in more noble perfection the qualities of greatness that marked his calm, cool, calculating intelligence and his big, brave bountiful heart," said the prelate. "Now, all of a sudden, he has been taken from us and, I dare say, we shall not see his like again.

"Who among us," the Cardinal said in slow, measured tones, "can forget those childish ways which, from time to time, enhanced the elegance of the executive mansion with the touching scenes of a happy family life! Charming Caroline 'stealing' the publicity; jovial John-John on all fours ascending the stairs of an airplane to greet his 'daddy,' and the loving mother, like all mothers, joyfully watching the two children of her flesh and blood, mindful always of three others in the nurseries of Heaven.

"At the side of the President, in understanding, devotion and affection, behold his gracious and beautiful Jacqueline!" the prelate said, asserting that "these days of sorrow must be more difficult for her than for any others but Divine Providence has blessed her, as few such women in history, by allowing her hero husband to have the dying comfort of her arms."

A few hours later, at Logan Airport, the Cardinal disclosed that he had advised the family to have the President buried in Arlington.

"It seemed to me that it was just not practical to have a national shrine here," he told reporters. "We faced the problem of bringing the body back to Massachusetts. The body would have been unburied another night, and then the family would have to endure another ceremony here.

"We all wanted to use common sense about the funeral," the Cardinal continued. "We decided on the shortest funeral mass, a low mass that will last only forty minutes. I didn't want the family to have to endure a long ceremony. A solemn high mass would run to at least an hour and a half."

The Washington service was held in St. Matthew's Cathedral, six blocks from the White House. It is a rather ugly, seventy-year-old red brick building with a dome 200 feet high. The Romanesque-Byzantine interior is decorated in pink Carrara marble and mosaics of Venetian glass.

Cardinal Cushing, vested in funeral garb, met the coffin at the door of the church. He sprinkled it with holy water and recited prayers. Then, he led the body down the aisle toward the altar, in the presence of members of Congress, foreign dignitaries and diplomats. The Kennedy family was seated in a special section down front. Across the aisle sat Lyndon Baines Johnson, the new 36th President of the United States, and Mrs. Johnson.

Just behind the new President were former Presidents Dwight D. Eisenhower and Harry S. Truman. Elsewhere in the cathedral were heads of state of many nations and of many faiths.

Caroline and John were seated beside their mother. John had been given a picture book to help keep him occupied. When he became restive, a Secret Service agent gently lifted him from the pew and took him outside. Later, he was on the front steps to execute the manly salute that made one of the lasting pictures of the ceremonies.

At 12:15 P.M., the white-haired Cardinal, wearing his scarlet skullcap, began chanting the ancient ritual in Latin. As he had promised, the mass was a low one, in that it was spoken instead of sung. Although the Boston cardinal was the only officiating clergyman, two other archbishops and four bishops were in the sanctuary during the rites.

"Make no mistake, brethren, about those who have gone to their rest," said Cardinal Cushing, reading from St. Paul's Epistle to the Thessalonians. "You are not to lament over them, as the rest of the world does, with no hope to live by. We believe that as Jesus underwent death and rose again, so God will bring back all those who have found rest through him. . . ."

When the Cardinal offered communion at the conclusion of the offertory, Jacqueline Kennedy rose quickly from her place, lifted her black veil from her face and walked steadily forward to the communion rail.

Robert Kennedy followed, with other members of the family, and then nearly 200 persons in all flocked to the rail from all parts of the cathedral to receive the wafer representing the body and blood of the risen Christ.

The Cardinal was assisted at the mass by the Rev. John F. Fitzgerald, of St. Jude's Parish in Norfolk, Massachusetts, a cousin of the late President. Within the sanctuary were Archbishop O'Boyle, who had returned the night before from the Vatican Council in Rome; Archbishop Egidio Vagnozzi, new Apostolic Delegate to the United States; Auxiliary Bishop Philip M. Hannon, of Washington, and Auxiliary Bishop John J. Maguire of New York, representing Cardinal Spellman.

There was no eulogy, in the accepted sense. But at the close of the mass, Bishop Hannan mounted the high marble pulpit and read several passages of Scripture which he said were favorites of the President. He also read the text of the Inaugural Address of 1961, with its challenge: "Ask not what your country can do for you; ask rather what you can do for your country."

Cardinal Cushing, moving down from the altar to pronounce absolution over the coffin, added a final prayer that appeared to be said on the spur of the moment, "May God, dear Jack, lead you into Paradise. May the martyrs receive you at your coming. May the spirit of God increase and mayest thou, for all who made the supreme sacrifice of dying for others, receive eternal rest in peace. Amen."

Wearing a white bishop's miter over the skullcap of his office, the Cardinal twice walked around the coffin, sprinkling it with holy water and perfuming it with incense.

The prelate then moved over to where the Kennedys were seated. He bent down and said a few words to Caroline and kissed her gently on the cheek. Jacqueline whispered to him, "Thanks, for calling him dear Jack."

The Cardinal again then led the coffin as it was rolled slowly out of the cathedral. Then, standing to one side until the coffin was brought down the 20 steps by the honor guard to the hearse, Cardinal Cushing bent down and kissed the coffin. With his handkerchief, he wiped tears from his eyes.

In brief ceremonies at the graveside in Arlington, the

Cardinal prayed, "Please, God, give us the grace to follow in the footsteps of the wonderful man we bury here today."

He again spoke to Jacqueline, then walked to the side of the grieving mother, Mrs. Rose Kennedy, embraced her—and walked away.

Time took up the thread swiftly. But instead of the usual festive occasion on Thanksgiving Day at Blinstrub's, back in South Boston, the Cardinal took the opportunity to pay deep personal tribute to the memory of the President and to his family for the assembled oldsters and handicapped. He recounted the scenes in the cathedral and Jacqueline's whispered message.

"There is a story in the Bible concerning a valiant woman," said the Cardinal. "That valiant woman in the Bible was reproduced in the twentieth century by Jacqueline Kennedy, wife of the late, beloved President."

Just before Christmas, Cardinal Cushing received a book from Jacqueline, entitled, *Inaugural Addresses of the United States, from George Washington, 1789, to John F. Kennedy, 1961.* The gift was leather-bound, gilt-edged and boxed. It was one of 85 copies that had been similarly published and bound by the U. S. Government Printing Office for the President to give to particular friends.

The inscription, in her hand, read:

> For your Eminence—Jack was going to give you this for Christmas. Pleace accept it now from me. With my devotion always—for all you were to our "dear Jack" and to me. Respectfully, Jackie.

On December 29, the Cardinal went to Palm Beach to celebrate a private mass at the winter home of Joseph P. Kennedy. He also spoke at a memorial mass for the late President in Miami.

In the Miami address, the Cardinal asserted that death had often brushed close to the President, "and it hovered near his patrol boat during the Second World War."

The prelate displayed a set of Navy dogtags worn by the President during the Pacific action. He said they had been given him by the President's widow, "and I promised her they would never get away from me."

In a brief press conference at Miami, the Cardinal called Jacqueline "the most extraordinary woman I have ever met."

"I wish I could say to the young girls of the future that I think instead of looking to motion picture actresses for ideals, they should look to Jacqueline Kennedy."

Some weeks later, on January 19, 1964, Cardinal Cushing stood on the front steps of the Cathedral of the Holy Cross in Boston and met Jacqueline Kennedy with outstretched hands. It was the occasion of a solemn pontifical mass that represented a blending of Boston's cultural and liturgical witness to the memory of John F. Kennedy.

Cardinal Cushing had joked at rehearsal the day before, offering to "take up the collection." But on this day, he was at his humble best. He took the arm of Jacqueline Kennedy and gently led her down the aisle of the huge edifice. So quietly was the entrance made that few were aware she had arrived and was kneeling in a front pew.

Six television cameras were focused on the proceedings at the altar, including one firmly planted in the pulpit. Miles of cable were snaked around corners to carry the ceremony to a watching nation. One battery of microphones encircled the 54-member Boston Symphony Orchestra for a stereophonic reproduction of Mozart's Requiem in D Minor.

Shortly after the service got under way, a light in a tier of lights over the main aisle sputtered and burned out, but few seemed to notice, so intent was the congregation on the successful combining of the mass with the music of chorus and choir, under Erich Leinsdorf's direction.

Jacqueline Kennedy, who had been dry-eyed throughout the funeral of her husband eight weeks earlier, wept silently as she listened to the mass. Tears flowed down her face as she went forward later to receive communion. Mrs. Rose Kennedy, Edward and other members of the family also were on hand and received the wafer from the hand of the prelate.

At the close of the mass, the Cardinal again moved to the lectern before the high altar. This time, he pleaded, "My few words will not, I hope, intrude on the solemnity of this occasion."

He expressed his gratitude to Henry Cabot for suggesting the use of the Symphony Orchestra in a civic ceremony. And he asserted that "the day has a special meaning for all of us, by the presence of the late President's wife, valiant Jacqueline, who has taken herself from her sorrow for a few hours to pray to God with us in sacrifice and song.

"We are grateful, too," he went on, "for the presence of the mother of our departed President, a resolute symbol of maternal strength, for the company of his brother and sisters and all of those of his family and friends who came from near and far to honor his memory still so fresh among us."

Asserting that "no one will fail to notice the appropriateness of selecting Mozart's Requiem," the Cardinal said, "Separated by centuries, these two men were touched by a creative instinct uncommon in any generation; both brought out of their youth a shining light which will illumine the ages; both were summoned to eternity at a moment which to mortals must seem untimely. Mozart died before he finished his immortal Requiem; President Kennedy died before he even finished his first term in office. Yet the memory of men will enshrine their names among the great of the world."

When he finished, Cardinal Cushing led Jacqueline and Rose Kennedy into the sanctuary to shake hands with Leinsdorf. Jacqueline whispered to the Cardinal, "It was magnificent. I will never forget it."

CHAPTER XVI

Current Issues:
Liberalism and the Right Wing

CARDINAL CUSHING's predilection for making off-hand remarks about current issues occasionally leaves him well out on a limb. Often these remarks concern political situations and they have sometimes led to contretemps which he might wisely have avoided.

An overall view of Cushing's opinions and activities as a public figure for a quarter of a century gives him an impressive stature as a liberal-minded man. He has always been an outspoken foe of Communism—hardly unexpected in a Roman Catholic prelate—but at the same time he has espoused causes which conservatives try to blight with the Communist label. His exhortations to tolerance are based on Christian doctrine and his own experience as a member of a barely tolerated minority. His practice of it has altered the religious atmosphere of Boston to provide increasing social and economic opportunities for Irish Catholics. Apart from his gregariousness, folksiness and interest in people of all sorts, which are perfectly genuine, he takes literally his obligations as shepherd of a flock in which class distinctions exist in spite of him. He spoke favorably of the late President Kennedy's far-reaching plans for a war on poverty; in general, despite the power and eminence of his position, he is egalitarian by temperament, unimpressed by social position, and on the side of democracy and the common man. In his zealous opposition to Communism in Latin America, he has shown an enlightened awareness of social conditions and class injustices which make it vulnerable to Communist influence.

It is one thing to form cordial ties with the Protestant and Jewish communities for the sake of better ecumenical relations. It takes a good deal more courage and conviction to support the cause of a dispossessed minority. Yet Cardinal Cushing is a life member of the N.A.A.C.P. and has been outspoken in favor of integration. If the religious climate of Boston is milder than it used to be, the racial climate is still stormy. The Boston school committee has refused to recognize that de facto segregation exists in the public schools. In protest, the Negro community in 1964, backed by many religious leaders and by civil rights groups, staged two stay-out demonstrations, in which the children remained out of public schools and attended "freedom" schools, where they sang and heard lectures on Negro history and racial problems.

The Cardinal, in a pastoral letter on interracial justice, said that "when a Catholic fails to take a stand against race intolerance and prejudice, he is a slacker in the army of the church militant." Yet when the Negroes announced their second stay-out, the prelate did not hesitate to call the movement "ill-advised." The Cardinal was not alone in his view. But when Dick Gregory, the noted Negro entertainer, expressed surprise, Cardinal Cushing was moved to issue a formal statement to explain his position.

The prelate said that he did not believe that such demonstrations would solve the problem, but rather "throw emotional obstacles in the way of expert study." He asserted that "children should be educated, not exhibited," and suggested neighborhood study halls where children could do their homework afternoons in peace and quiet, if such conditions did not exist at home. The stay-out demonstration went on anyway, although there were no incidents.

At about the same time, a controversy arose all over the country when Rolf Hochhuth's play *The Deputy* opened in New York. The play was based on the supposition that Pope Pius XII, who was Pontiff during World War II, had not done all that he might have done to prevent the persecution and the extermination of Jews by the Nazis. It brought a storm of protest from the Roman Catholic Church, much of it intemperate. In contrast, the official word of the Boston Archdiocese, as voiced by the *Pilot,* was notably mild. While it called the play the "posthumous abuse of petty partisans attempting to defame" the memory of Pope Pius XII, it did not devote the entire article to denunciation. In view of Cardinal Cushing's later acts on behalf of the Jews, and the part that the German Cardinal Bea played in supporting them, the *Pilot*'s comment seemed to have a special significance:

> If the play causes us to look again into our hearts and weigh the actions of all of us in those awful hours, it can be said to have at least one salutary effect. The Christians of Germany and of the whole world, as well as so many others, have scarcely begun the examination of conscience that history will eventually demand.

In view of the progressive attitudes he has displayed, and of his avoidance of extremism, the Cardinal's occasional support of right-wingers has baffled many Catholics. Although he did not explicitly endorse Joseph McCarthy, his unflagging hatred of Communism led him to condone the tactics of the flamboyant Wisconsin Republican in a way that seemed to indicate his support of him. As Archbishop during the McCarthy era, he suggested that if there were some other answer to Communism besides the McCarthy assault, "I'm for that, too."

Senator Joseph R. McCarthy emerged on the public scene early in 1950 as a self-appointed foe of Communism. In a Lincoln Day speech in Wheeling, West Virginia, one night in February of that year, McCarthy held aloft a sheaf of paper, which, he croaked hoarsely, bore the names of 150 Communists in the State Department. Although assigned there as a run-of-the-mill speaker in a second-rate state for Republicans, the Wisconsin Senator struck a spark in a powder keg of public sentiment that skyrocketed him into undreamed-of fame. It did not matter that he never proved his contention. As a Roman Catholic layman, the black-browed Irishman became an overnight hero in cities like Boston. It was not like damning England, but it would do.

Whatever importance history may assign to him later, McCarthy became the symbol of smear, distortion and self-aggrandizement in his day, appealing to mass emotion rather than to reason until his own colleagues in the United States Senate censured him. And until he began to take himself more seriously than his cause, criticism of Joe McCarthy in Boston could earn the critic a punch in the nose. In some sections, it still can.

Against that background, Archbishop Cushing was asked

his opinion of McCarthyism during a homeward voyage on the Cunard liner *Queen Mary* in September of 1953. He replied, "It all depends on what they think of Communism. Despite any extremes or mistakes that may have been made, I don't believe anything has brought out the evils and methods of Communism more to the American people than the investigations." The Boston prelate did not elaborate on extremes or mistakes.

A year later, the Archbishop was asked to comment on the Army-McCarthy controversy, an investigation of the Senator's charges against individual officers. His attention was called to a speech by Senator Ralph E. Flanders, Republican of Vermont, asserting that Senator McCarthy was dividing the country, his church and his party by his slurs.

The Vermonter had noted that although Francis Cardinal Spellman of New York had shaken hands with McCarthy after a speech in New York, Bishop Bernard J. Sheil of Chicago had condemned the Wisconsin Republican's activities.

"He certainly is not dividing the church," asserted Archbishop Cushing. "There is no Catholic attitude on the issue and Catholics can go the way they will."

Even before McCarthy disappeared from the spotlight, the victim of hepatitis, Robert H. W. Welch, a North Carolina descendant of a family of Baptist ministers, was already in the wings awaiting a cue.

Welch, with his brother James, had parlayed a hole-in-the-wall fudge factory in Cambridge, Massachusetts, into a lucrative candy business, through the simple expedient of arranging to have their goods displayed in supermarkets, near the check-out counters, where hungry housewives, or their children, would notice them and reach.

Welch, probably with sincere motives aroused by the turmoil of the times, entered the Republican campaign for the nomination of lieutenant governor of Massachusetts in 1950. He bought newspaper advertising space liberally to thunder against encroaching socialism in government and abroad. In the primary, he ran a respectable third in the field of five.

From then on, Welch devoted more and more time to speaking, traveling and writing about the evils of socialism. At length, he resigned from the Welch Candy Company and became a crusader. In 1954, he published a biography of John Birch.

John Birch, a Baptist missionary who was born on a farm in Macon, Georgia, was in China when World War II broke out. Enlisting with General Clare Chennault's intelligence forces as a volunteer, Birch rose to the rank of captain before the conflict ended.

Ten days after the Japanese surrender, in August, 1945, John Birch, still in uniform on a government mission for the United States, was slain by Chinese Communists, according to the Welch biography. The biography said that "the Communists in Washington" tried to hide the incident, but that Senator William Knowland, Republican of California, and Birch's parents succeeded in piercing the "blanket of oblivion."

Welch founded the John Birch Society in Indianapolis on December 9, 1958. The basic document of the society was a private letter from Welch to a group of acquaintances setting forth his views on patriotic values. As he later related the story, the letter was continually revised and more widely distributed until it ran to 80,000 words. It became known as the Blue Book. Among other things, it branded President Eisenhower as a "dedicated Communist."

The society was set up to operate through local chapters of 10 to 20 members each. It had an immediate appeal to those of ultra-conservative views, a great many of them lonely women and retired military men.

From the outset, Welch made it clear that the society was monolithic, and as its numbers grew to an estimated 100,-000, he began tilting, in McCarthy fashion, with anyone who questioned his methods. Before long, the society launched a campaign to impeach Chief Justice Earl Warren for treason.

Society members were encouraged among other things to run for school committees in order to exercise censorship over textbooks to be used in the public schools. Letter-writing campaigns aimed at congressmen and editors were other tactics.

On April 28, 1960, before the Birch venom had spread very far, Archbishop Cushing, in answer to a query from C. M. Crawford of Los Angeles, wrote:

> Replying to your recent letter, I beg to advise you that I do not know of any more dedicated anti-Communist in the country than Robert Welch. I unhesitatingly recommend him to you and endorse his John Birch Society. Under separate cover I am sending you some literature that may be of interest to you.

About four years later, in a speech in Sudbury, Massachusetts, before a Protestant audience, Cardinal Cushing commented that he knew Welch, "a good Baptist, who had gone to extremes occasionally, but the present Communist secondary line is to back that group and many similar groups."

Then, on the evening of April 19, 1964, a Sunday, the prelate found a telegram awaiting him when he returned to his residence after a busy day. The message asked him if he endorsed the John Birch Society and, by inference, statements that Presidents Franklin D. Roosevelt and Kennedy were Communists. It was signed "Gretchen van Heussen," who purported to be a correspondent in New York for Swiss and Italian newspapers.

Although the Cardinal did not disclose the entire contents, he said two members of the society apparently had made the charges on a radio program originating in New York and carried in Boston on Station WNAC. The program was identified as the *Long John Nebel Show*, an all-night discussion program from Station WOR.

Cardinal Cushing shook off his weariness, telephoned WNAC and demanded equal time. The diocesan news bureau was set to work on what proved to be a fruitless effort to find a Gretchen van Heussen.

The Cardinal appeared at the WNAC studios the following afternoon as a special guest on the Heywood Vincent show, a local discussion program, to assert that it was "a colossal lie" to suggest that he had endorsed the notion that either President was a Communist.

In measured tones of suppressed rage the Cardinal said:

"I never met President Roosevelt. I am proud to add, however, that I knew the late President Kennedy better than any member of the John Birch Society and all of them put together.

"If it is true that two members of this society called my nearest and dearest friend, the late John F. Kennedy, a Communist, they and their associates owe the people of all nations who loved him and who will never forget his tragic death a profound apology.

"If it is also true that two members of the Birch Society identified me with such an incredible remark, I cannot dig-

SALT OF THE EARTH

nify them with an answer save to say—shame, shame, shame
for attempting to blight the character and mar the memory
of a martyr to his country with that of a traitor."

The angry Cardinal said that his letter of endorsement
of four years earlier had been exploited in the West, but
not in the East "for the expansion of the John Birch Society, which I do not now endorse or approve. On the contrary, I do not want my name to be identified with it in any
way.

"In justice to myself and lest anyone be misled by my
silence," said the prelate, "I now retract publicly that letter
and especially its reference to the John Birch Society.

"This retraction is long overdue but I have been waiting
for the day when members of the Birch Society would ex-
tend their propaganda by the use of my name to this part
of the country."

The reaction was immediate. The Birch Society, through
Welch, said the telegram to the Cardinal contained "out-
right falsehoods." Scott Stanley, Jr., editor of *American
Opinion* magazine, a Birch publication, and Tom Davis, a
coordinator for the magazine, denied having called either
President a Communist. It developed that in answer to a
direct question by Mr. Nebel concerning endorsement by
any clergyman of the society, they had named Cardinal
Cushing.

The discussion also had touched on an article in the February, 1964, issue of *American Opinion* which said that
President Kennedy had collaborated with Premier Nikita
Khrushchev to stage a "sham" embargo of Cuba. It also asserted that President Kennedy had become a "political liability" to the Communist conspiracy in the United States
and so had been assassinated.

The writer of the telegram, apparently aware of remarks

218

about Presidents Kennedy and Roosevelt in other Birch Society publications, had lumped together a series of charges by implication.

By Thursday, having pieced together the major pieces of the story, the Cardinal publicly did an about-face. He asserted that he apparently had been led into his condemnation of the Birchers by a hoax and that many of his statements were unjustified and the result of misunderstanding. He authorized the Society to publish a letter of apology, which he had written and had handed to Davis. But what the public did not know was that Davis visited the Cardinal at his residence, explaining that he was a practicing Roman Catholic, that much of what had been imputed was by inference and that as a Catholic, he was embarrassed by the incident.

The Cardinal's letter read:

> Developments since my statements on the Heywood Vincent program have convinced me that I was misinformed as to what had been said on your own broadcast. Also, my memory was at fault concerning my letter of April 28, 1960, to Mr. Crawford. Since I did not specifically state in that letter that it was not to be published, permission certainly could have been implied.
>
> My statements were made with an if, and were conditional on the accuracy of the information I had received. Under the circumstances, I now feel that many of them were unjustified. Because of my own dedication to the fight against the atheistic Communist conspiracy, I certainly do not want to do any harm to fellow battlers in the same cause.
>
> While I think the Crawford letter is now too out of date for continued use, therefore, I would be glad to have Mr. Welch print this letter in his Bulletin of the John Birch Society if he wishes to do so.

And with my regret at the temporary worry caused many good people by the hoax perpetrated on me, I send you and your associates all good wishes and kind regards.

The episode left loyal Catholics shaking their heads in perplexity. Cardinal Cushing is not unaware of his own influence nor ignorant of the ways of politics; his statements and actions on behalf of many progressive causes have been deliberate and moderate. In the case of the John Birch Society—which condemns many of the causes and principles which the Cardinal supports—they seem ill informed and motivated only by his abhorrence of Communism rather than the thoughtfulness that characterizes his other political positions.

CHAPTER XVII

Silver Jubilee

THE year 1964 was Silver Jubilee year of Richard Cushing's consecration as a bishop, and coincided with the twentieth year of his personal administration of the archdiocese. He had emerged in the full flower of a legend. Exposure on television as part of the John F. Kennedy saga had widened his influence on a national scale. And his role as a leading spokesman of the progressives at the third session of the Vatican Council had thrust him on the international stage and assured him a place in Church history; how large a place would be determined by the span of years left to him, and by the cumulative effects of the Council on Church renewal.

Richard Cushing apparently has enjoyed all of this, aware that his comments occasionally have embroiled him in controversy and that his offhand manner sometimes has puzzled his own flock, who, having become a force in the community, no longer support the historic Catholic image of complete acquiescence to clerical pronouncements, including his. History also may determine whether Cushing forced some issues through the power of his intellect, or whether he actually was an instinctive opportunist, who knew when to move with the times.

Protestants have come to see him as a man with undaunted pride in his working-class, immigrant background. And, in the main, they have come to respect him for being himself and for his defense of anyone who has been the victim of bigotry or intolerance, even though some of his views have seemed to be old-fashioned. An unsolved mystery among Protestants as well as Catholics is the Cardinal's actual power. Let some public issue move into the spotlight, involving the need for some sort of leadership, and the question is posed, "What's the word from Lake Street?" the popular term for the archdiocesan chancery. But, aside from questions dealing with moral issues, the evidence is that the chancery waits for the power of public opinion to sway men's minds.

The Cardinal himself has admitted his influence on legislation. He has said that in an effort to bolster the regular congregation at the cathedral, he once urged legislation leading to the construction of a low-income housing project in the immediate neighborhood.

"And then," he commented, "the tenants turned out to be largely Negro Protestants!"

Whatever it was that put across legislation guaranteeing tax concessions to the Prudential Life Insurance Company of America during the construction period of its multimillion-dollar business center in the Back Bay district, there was no denying that the Cardinal was instrumental in selling the importance of the project to the community.

After Prudential had sunk $13,000,000 in foundation work on the site, a moment of doubt began to stretch into months of uncertainty. Its administrators reasoned that politicians might make sincere promises of cooperation, but that the attrition of the ballot box also could remove them from power before such promises could be met.

With that in mind, Prudential sought legislative guarantees. And at an appropriate moment, Cardinal Cushing asserted that the insurance center represented "a new lease on the economic life" of Boston. The bill passed. Yet it was evident that much of the groundwork had been done long before. Fred Smith, a Prudential vice-president, and the Cardinal had had many personal, unofficial conferences in the spirit of what the prelate asserted was that of "old friends."

And, in a later defense of legislators in general, the Cardinal asserted that no politician had sought any favors in connection with that particular project. And he probably was right; Massachusetts politicians may not take dictation from the Roman Catholic prelate, but they don't deliberately cross him.

If the Cardinal and the Catholic community of Boston wield a noticeable economic and political power, in the sphere of "Society" the changes are equally marked. Where once the Lowells spoke only to Cabots and the Cabots spoke only to God, the Shapiros, the Foleys and the Bartelletas speak to Cabots and Lowells about urban renewal; and they also go to one another's churches on appropriate occasions. The Boston Social Register is still filled with such names as Lowell, Cabot, Forbes, Adams, Frothingham, Saltonstall and Gardner; but there are also some Collinses, MacFaddens, Cahills and Darmodys. Once, it took two or three generations to make the Social Register; now, under proper circumstances, it can be done in one. Proper Protestant Boston has its June Cotillion, where fewer than one hundred debutantes are presented; and the Debutante Assembly at Thanksgiving, which is somewhat less exclusive. But since 1957 new generations of Catholic girls have had their own coming-out event, the Cardinal's St. Nicholas Cotillion during the Christmas holidays.

The private largesse of old Boston established the Boston Symphony, the Massachusetts General Hospital and the Perkins Institution for the Blind. The Irish, with the disadvantage of having had to start from scratch, have found that Cardinal Cushing offers an impressive list of social agencies that receive financial support from the Catholic community. St. Elizabeth's is the prelate's own hospital and a counterpart of the Massachusetts General, while the Carney and Bon Secours are Catholic-operated hospitals in the tradition of the Peter Bent Brigham or Massachusetts Memorials.

But where the older institutions had the benefit of generous individual endowments, many of the Catholic agencies have been supported by church-directed guilds embracing all manner of vocations, from telephone workers to doctors.

Each of the guilds contributes as generously as its individual members can afford to, even if it is a matter of 50 cents a month.

In education, the rolls of Radcliffe, Wellesley, Smith and Mount Holyoke still abound with Anglo-Saxon names, but such Catholic institutions as Emmanuel and Regis have a status of their own. And while Harvard continues to set the pace of acceptance and leadership on an international scale, some of the coming leaders of the new Boston are proud to be alumni of Boston College and Holy Cross.

A few Brahmins remain on the political scene. They include such names as Senator Leverett Saltonstall, Ambassador Henry Cabot Lodge and, in a sense, Christian A.

Herter, all Republicans, and Governor Endicott Peabody, a Democrat. They are matched nationally by House Speaker John W. McCormack, an Irish Catholic from South Boston.

It may have been indicative of changing times when John F. Kennedy defeated Henry Cabot Lodge for the Senate in 1952 in Massachusetts and prevailed again over him, nationally, in the Presidential race of 1960, when Mr. Lodge was the Republican Vice-Presidential nominee. And although the grief-stricken Cardinal said, after the assassination of President Kennedy, that his like would not be seen again, the growing stature of Senator Edward M. (Ted) Kennedy indicates that the place of Irish Catholics in the political and social structure of Boston is secure.

All these changes have taken place in the relatively brief time since Richard Cushing was a schoolboy in South Boston, to which he frequently returns.

In recognition of the twenty-fifth year of his consecration, Cardinal Cushing visited his native parish, Gate of Heaven, South Boston, to ordain two deacons to the priesthood. It was Gate of Heaven's first ordination service in the parish church since its founding in 1869. But only one of the two new priests was a native of the parish. The other was from neighboring Dorchester. The following day, the Cardinal was to ordain 23 others at the cathedral, in keeping with the general custom. He took the occasion in South Boston to express his regret at not being able to ordain at least 100 priests for his Jubilee.

But if vocations among younger men were falling off, there was a significant upsurge for vocations among older men. In a characteristic, seemingly offhand remark in 1960, in Marlboro, Massachusetts, Cardinal Cushing had said that he planned to erect a seminary for delayed vocations, in connection with a new parish church in that city. The Marlboro plan failed to materialize, but by 1963, a seminary building was rising in Weston, Massachusetts, about twelve miles west of Boston. It was named for Pope John.

An entering class of 54 inaugurated the seminary program in the fall of 1964. Monsignor George A. Schlichte, former rector of the North American College in Rome, was named rector of the new seminary. Many of the applicants had military backgrounds, dating from World War II. The first to be accepted was Richard F. Gardner, forty-seven years old, a native of Buffalo, New York. After service with the Air Force and sixteen years with American Airlines as a pilot instructor and executive, Mr. Gardner decided on holy orders when the seminary became available.

The candidates are to be trained as diocesan priests during a four-year course that will give them Latin enough to conduct services, and other studies, including theology, to qualify them for parish assignments. A parish church, associated with the seminary, will give them practical lessons in ministering to a congregation.

Shortly before his visit to his old home district, Cardinal Cushing found himself lunching with more than 200 Episcopal clerics at fashionable Trinity Church, in Copley Square. After the meal, he spoke for more than an hour and a half, alternately titillating and awing his audience with a mixture of wit and prayer for understanding.

After the meeting the Cardinal was shown around the church by the Rev. Dr. Theodore P. Ferris, rector of Trinity. Together, they knelt for a few moments in meditation in the main body of the church.

It was only one of many appearances which the Cardinal made at the religious services of other faiths, expressing pleasure at the progress of the second session of the Vatican

Council, where he had stayed two weeks, and emphasizing the "springtime spirit of new discovery of one another and of wonder at the myriad links which bind us together after centuries of separation."

But with all his established position in the upper circles of Boston and his new international eminence as a cardinal, his love of children and of "little people" remains his most compelling quality as a churchman. He returned to South Boston to celebrate a solemn requiem mass for Nora Harrington, who had died at the age of eighty-nine, having outlived her husband Tim, a piano tuner, by twenty years.

Although it is no longer customary to give eulogies, the Cardinal made an exception for Nora. He said:

"For forty years, Nora greeted me at the door of this church when I came here on assignment. For all my work with the missions, I believe this little woman did more. She died penniless, but deep in our affection and with the richest treasure known to man, she died in the love of God.

"And what would delight Nora most is all the attention she is getting. A Prince of the Church in his scarlet robes, five monsignori and a dozen priests have come to pay her honor.

"Today, I welcome Nora to the church for the last time. I am honoring myself more than her memory in being here."

Nora was said to have been deeply stirred by the Cushing sermons on missions, when he preached on the works of the Propagation Society; either that, or she had a soft spot for him because he came from South Boston. In any event, for forty years, Nora Harrington was reported to have managed to send $25 a month to the "Propie Society," as she called it. And she saw to it that masses were said for the departed and that the mass stipends were collected.

To prove she knew the Cardinal, Nora showed her neighbors letters that began "Dear Nora," and were signed "Richard Cardinal Cushing." Some of her friends teased her, suggesting she had written them herself. But about three years before she died, her big moment came. The Cardinal was at St. Vincent's for confirmation. An eyewitness recalled the scene.

"Himself came out of the church, with his miter high on his head, swinging his brass walking stick. Down the steps he came, dignified as the high altar. Then he spotted Nora in the crowd across the street.

" 'Hello, Nora!' says the Cardinal. He strode across E Street and put his arms around her and gave her a big hug.

" 'It wouldn't be St. Vincent's without seeing you,' himself said, and everyone around heard him."

All the way home, Nora said to herself, "Now they'll believe me." And from then on, they did.

The Cardinal has little use for personal anniversaries unless he can turn them to account for his charity funds. Nor does he mind making informal comments on conventionally solemn occasions. At a speech at a high school commencement recently, he said, "I have attended many commencements. I don't remember a word any commencement speaker ever said, and I don't remember anything I ever said. . . ."

At a dinner in honor of his birthday, he said, "Don't try to guess how old I am because I don't really know." This was true; one birth record shows his birth date as August 23, 1895, and another August 24.

Nevertheless he celebrated his sixty-eighth birthday by inviting 250 old people from Little Sisters of the Poor homes in Roxbury and Somerville to go to Paragon Park, a seaside amusement center in Hull. For four hours, he hopped from table to table, sang songs, poured beer, bit the ends off cigars and lit them. Then he took a roller coaster ride with twelve frightened nuns. All, including the Cardinal, blessed themselves beforehand.

A bystander at the finish reported that a young nun sitting beside the prelate tried to apologize for having gripped his arm so tightly during the ride.

"Aw, forget it, Sister, I'm old enough to be your father!" the Cardinal exclaimed.

Later, coming upon a mallet-swinging concession with a sign reading, HOW STRONG ARE YOU? the Cardinal seized the heavy tool and shot the striker gong-high to register, STRONG AS A TRUCK DRIVER.

At the restaurant, the guests, ranging from seventy to ninety-eight, sang "Happy Birthday." The Cardinal, who had been wearing a waiter's cap most of the time, suddenly plunked his own straw boater on the head of Mrs. Elizabeth Ford, eighty-five years old, and clowned around with her hat on his head. Since it was Friday, the prelate dispensed all hands from abstaining from meat, but quipped, "The die-hards can still have fish chowder."

After rounding up two priests and one professional entertainer, the Cardinal organized a barbershop quartet to sing old favorites. Finally he said, "Have you had enough penance, or do you want more?" They took some more.

The Cardinal rode in one of the chartered buses both ways, pointing out landmarks. At one spot, he commented, "Ah, here we are in good Old Southie, and there's Columbia Point, the Globe and B. C. High."

The Christmas following the assassination of President Kennedy, the Cardinal was grieving with the rest of the nation but he kept to his tradition of visiting shut-ins. This time, it was City Hospital. Wearing street clericals instead of his cassock, he played and joked with the patients.

He picked up a two-year-old girl, who had been abandoned. She was known to the hospital only as "Baby X." The child cried at being lifted.

"I'm not very good at this stuff," the Cardinal said, handing the baby back to a nurse, "but it is an honor in itself, holding a baby."

He stopped off to autograph a Bible for a sixteen-year-old boy, who had been hospitalized for five months after an abdominal operation. He next strolled into a ward and surprised half a dozen men.

"Hope I didn't break up a crap game," he said chuckling.

After the Cardinal had swept through another area, one little old lady said, "It's the Cardinal in person; I saw him face to face."

A two-and-a-half-year-old Negro youngster didn't want to eat his ice cream for his nurse. But when she was replaced by a strange man, wearing a fascinating ring on his right hand, the boy looked around in wonder.

"Pay no attention to them," said the Cardinal, indicating his entourage of photographers. "Just eat." And he did.

Several times, as he walked into wards, the Cardinal exclaimed, "Relax, I am not going to take up a collection."

But between times, he became completely serious in the face of the desperately ill and imparted a Latin blessing.

And there was another little, old lady who said to him, "I can't sleep very good."

The Cardinal gave her a smile of deep sympathy and said, "My dear, neither can I."

A few months later, Cardinal Cushing visited the Soldiers' Home in Chelsea, Massachusetts. He was greeted by an honor guard of Fourth Degree Knights of Columbus, in their plumed hats and bearing ceremonial swords. But he spotted smudge-faced Joe Delaney, two and a half years old, outside the chapel, took him by the hand and marched him down the center aisle to a pew to pray.

Joe's delighted mother took a snapshot outside, but she whispered to someone nearby, "Oh, my, he's so grubby." But aside from that little smudge on his face, Joe didn't look grubby to anyone else who witnessed the scene.

In the hospital, the prelate knelt beside the bed of Jacob Mulsman, seventy-two years old, and sang a duet from World War I, " 'Til We Meet Again."

"I'm celebrating the Passover with the best Jew in Boston," laughed the Cardinal at the end.

"Who is he?" asked Mulsman.

"You," said the Cardinal, "and God bless you."

"Okay, kid," replied Mulsman.

At another bed, learning that a grandnephew of ninety-one-year-old John McCarthy was soon to be ordained, Cardinal Cushing said, "I'll give him permission to say mass right here at the foot of the bed, facing you, and if he can't do it, I'll come myself."

Amid such homely activities, the Cardinal also was host to three visiting dignitaries of the Church, all of them known as liberals: Cardinals Koenig of Austria and Suenens of Belgium, who came to lecture under the auspices of the Paulist Fathers, and Cardinal Bea, the eighty-three-year-old German—a staunch advocate of the Jews—whose subsequent return to Boston to receive a degree from Harvard University gave rise to speculation that he was also visiting the Boston cardinal on a secret mission related to the forthcoming third session of the Vatican Council. On Bea's second visit, Cardinal Cushing hinted that something was in the wind; Cardinal Bea was met by photographers and reporters. Harvard University, according to custom, made no comment. Cardinal Bea spent several days with Cushing, then departed almost secretly; the local news desks received no advance notice of his leaving.

On each arrival, the Cardinal was on hand to greet the visitor personally. As he was walking with Franz Cardinal Koenig through the airport, he spotted a man hurrying past. The Boston prelate reached out and grabbed the man's arm, saying, "Here, say hello to Cardinal Koenig."

When the man protested that he had a plane to catch, the Cardinal assured him it would only take a minute.

The man then said, "But I'm not a Catholic!"

"So much the better," said Cardinal Cushing, and after a brief handclasp the man sped on. Leon Joseph Cardinal Suenens of Brussels arrived with somewhat less fanfare, although the Boston prelate gave him a wrestler's hug for the benefit of photographers.

No fanfare attended Richard Cushing's departure for the third session of the Vatican Council. In fact, he was in Rome almost before he was missed in diocesan circles in Boston. He had his chauffeur drive him to New York and booked passage on the first available flight to Rome. This was a new Cushing, who bore little resemblance to the puckish prelate who liked to tell audiences that he gave up listening to the first two sessions of the Council because he couldn't understand the Latin. This time, the Boston cardinal apparently realized that the hour had come for him to make his move and he flew straight on to his new rendez-vous with history.

Twice, during the three weeks he spent in Rome this

time, Cardinal Cushing rose before his peers in St. Peter's Basilica and pleaded—in eloquent Latin—for exoneration of the Jews of the blame for Christ's Crucifixion and for religious freedom of all mankind. The gravelly voice had heavy overtones of Bostonese but its ring prompted the listening bishops to break the rules by applauding vigorously. And when he finally returned home, Richard Cushing again flew to New York, where his car picked him up for the last leg of the journey to Boston. Although New York reporters assigned to the airport beat managed to intercept him briefly, the Cardinal said he was not at liberty to tell them why he had returned early, and that he had landed in New York to avoid meeting the press of his own city.

But Cushing's appearance in Rome was more than a hurried visit to speak his piece and then retreat from the scene of a quiet revolution. The Cardinal played one of the leading roles in that third act of the Council. In retrospect it appeared that he had been well coached in his lines by the liberal cardinals from Europe who had visited Boston in the preceding two years.

The last foreign prelate to visit Boston before Cushing's trip to Rome had been Archbishop Dino Staffa, secretary of the Sacred Congregation of Seminaries and Universities, and a leading conservative. But if in fact he tried to dissuade the Bostonian from taking part in the liberal movement, he came too late with too little.

It had been apparent from the first session that most of the American and Northern European bishops were not going to Rome merely for the ride. They interpreted Pope John's call for a cleansing breeze through the fusty corridors of the Church as a movement to bring it into the nuclear age of the twentieth century, and they had no intentions of becoming rubber stamps for the entrenched Curia of Italian cardinals who handled administrative functions of the Holy See.

A few bishops, including many conservatives from Middle Europe, had the oversimplified notion that since the Pope was infallible in pronouncement on faith and morals, he did not need them in such matters. This wing believed the chief function of a bishop was to do what he was told, to deliver the papal message to his people, to continue building churches and schools, and to preach the Gospel, as he had been taught years before in seminary.

Pope Paul eventually stepped on the conservatives. He showed deep concern in the ecumenical movement begun by his predecessor and left hope for further advances by indicating that a fourth session would be held. He apparently was aware, also, of the rapid turn of events in the secular world between the second and third sessions—the assassination of President John F. Kennedy, Cardinal Cushing's friend, bringing changes in the Administration in Washington, as well as changes that were in the making in London and in Moscow.

Richard Cushing had already said that the whole Council would "fall flat on its face" if it did not approve a statement on religious freedom. So, under his leadership, 170 of the 240 United States prelates met on September 17 at the North American College in Rome and decided not only to press for the religious freedom pronouncement but also to strengthen the official position on exoneration of the Jews. And with an eye to becoming bishops in fact as well as in name, they agreed also to work for collegial, or collective rule, as partners of the Pope.

Cushing was elected to plead the cause of the progressives on religious liberty. He faced opposition from Alfredo

Cardinal Ottaviani, secretary of the Holy Office, who had become the symbol of archconservatism. Ottaviani urged the primacy of supernatural rights, the Church's claim to absolute knowledge of religious truth, over the natural right of freedom of conscience.

The progressive declaration was drafted by the Vatican Secretariat for the Promotion of Christian Unity, whose director was Cardinal Bea. It held that each man had an obligation to seek out knowledge of the law of God, and it asserted the belief that the Roman Catholic Church was the pure expression of God's will. But, in a revolutionary formulation, it stated that a man acting in sincere obedience to his conscience was implicitly obeying the divine law. The document asserted that "if in his attempts to know the will of God, a man falls into an erroneous interpretation of that will, no man and no power has the right to induce him to act contrary to the dictate of his conscience." Projecting that individual right into the field of organized religion, the draft also declared the freedom of religious groups. This freedom, the progressive view contended, could be restricted legitimately only when it was in grave conflict with the ends of society.

In support of these concepts, Cardinal Cushing said that approval of them was important to safeguard what had been well called in the American Declaration of Independence "a decent respect for the opinion of mankind." And he referred also to the British historian, Lord Acton, who had held that "freedom is the highest political end." The seventy-three-year-old Ottaviani, with the tut-tutting manner of conservatives, asserted that those professing revealed religion had rights over and above those coming from the natural law. And he declared firmly, "We must profess and defend our Catholic faith no matter what happens." And although Pope Paul eventually overrode the objections of 1,000 progressives for a final vote at the third session, it was apparent that the matter of religious freedom would have top priority at a fourth session.

As the progressive movement began to surge during the third session, the gentle-appearing but shrewd Bea pushed for a revision of the text on the Jews. Before the session closed on November 21, the Bea forces prevailed, even though official promulgation of the Jewish exoneration would have to await the fourth session.

Once again, Cardinal Cushing was in the forefront of the progressive march. "Far be it from us to set ourselves up in the place of God as judges," he told the 2,000 prelates in St. Peter's. And although he had returned home long before the final settlement of the issue, he had the satisfaction of knowing how strong was the support for his view. At length, the Council held that "the Jewish people should never be presented as one rejected, cursed or guilty of deicide."

"What happened to Christ in His Passion," said the declaration, "cannot be attributed to the whole people then alive, much less to that of today. Besides, the Church held and holds that Christ underwent His Passion and death freely, because of the sins of all men and out of infinite love."

While this was an important step, there still remained references to "perfidious Jews" and other phrases in Scripture, liturgy and catechism reflecting the old attitude. Pope John had ordered out of the Good Friday "prayer of intercession for the Jews" language that might be offensive. This left it up to Pope Paul, among other important decisions, to revise other Catholic writings in the same vein.

In another historic advance, the Council gave final approval to collegial relationship between the Pope and the bishops.

The Council's vote to replace Latin with modern languages in much of the liturgy went into effect, November 29, 1964. But Cardinal Cushing, exerting his prerogative as primate of New England, used the English form in a memorial mass for President Kennedy on November 22, the first anniversary of his assassination.

Not the least of the modernizing steps was the re-establishment of a permanent order of deacons, a sort of lesser priesthood to aid in pastoral duties and missionary work where ordained priests were scarce. The function had atrophied in recent centuries to a title devolving on seminarians as an intermediate step toward full priesthood. The measure broke with the absolute clerical celibacy dating from the eleventh century. Celibacy was to remain in effect for younger men, but married men of mature years might be eligible for the diaconate.

When the possibility of this step was brought up some time before the Council, Cardinal Cushing commented drolly, "Then the bishops would run the Church, the priests would do all the work and the deacons would have all the fun!"

The idea of a diaconate, a recognized rank in the Episcopal Church, for example, and the use of what amounted to lay readers—a tradition dating back to Judaism—in certain lessons of the mass, were understandable to most Protestants. What puzzled them still was Pope Paul's firm declaration that Mary was the Mother of the Church. The question of Mary's place in theology has long been a stumbling block to understanding between Catholics and Protestants. The Pope's reaffirmation of her position as Mother of the Church indicated that Cardinal Cushing had been right in telling Protestant audiences that the full reunion of Christendom might have to await the end of time.

But of the ecumenical significance of the Council's declaration on Jews there was no doubt. The reaction in the Jewish community to Cardinal Cushing's pressing the Vatican Council for a declaration absolving Jews of the Crucifixion of Jesus Christ was one of rejoicing. In Boston Dr. Alexander Brin, the scholarly editor and publisher of the weekly *Jewish Advocate,* "nominated" the prelate for a Nobel Prize in recognition of his efforts. In a speech to a suburban Rotary Club, Dr. Brin asserted that the Cardinal's "magnificent call at the Ecumenical assembly has evoked a deep, reverberating echo in humanity's collective heart.

"He gave a living demonstration as a great human being who possesses the moral power and spiritual idealism of such immortals as Roger Williams, Thomas Jefferson and Abraham Lincoln. He deserves the Nobel Prize for meritorious service in behalf of peace and goodwill," said the Jewish editor.

"Rarely has a religious leader of any denomination in this country won such a commanding position in the life of the nation and won the universal regard of leaders in all creeds, as well as the respect of millions of their followers as has Cardinal Cushing."

Rabbi Joseph S. Shubow of Temple B'nai Moshe, virtually a neighbor of the Cardinal, told his congregation in a special Thanksgiving sermon that "for the gallant step forward and for the marshaling of the hosts in the name of human freedom, we must ever be thankful to the American

hierarchy in general and to Boston's most distinguished citizen, Cardinal Cushing, in particular."

On his return from Rome, Cardinal Cushing, caught up
in the whirl of diocesan affairs, had little to say publicly
about his nineteen days at the third session of the Council.
And, of course, no one in Boston pressed him, knowing that
he kept his own counsel in such matters. But to the
daughter of a California rabbi, Trude B. Feldman, the
correspondent of *The Jewish Press*, a New York weekly,
the Cardinal pointed out that no one could say that the Jews
alone were guilty of deicide.

"Who killed Christ?" he asked. "Whether it was the Ro-
mans or others we don't know, but the point is we can't
change history. We can't change what is recorded in the
Gospel. All of us—Jews and Gentiles, everyone—crucified
Christ, because He chose to die for all our sins, to make
atonement for our sins.

"I am hopeful my good Jewish friends throughout the
country will be satisfied with the declaration from the Ecumenical Council. No one went as far as I did on behalf of
the Jews and I'm tremendously fond of the Jews and they
of me. I've received thouands of letters from Jews all over
the world on my statements at the Ecumenical Council.

"I did not make those statements in any special effort to
befriend the Jews. They can take care of themselves, just as
I can take care of myself."

Although the Cardinal did not immediately plunge back
into his round of visits to Protestant churches, he sent Auxiliary Bishop Thomas J. Riley to Christ Episcopal Church
in Cambridge to represent him at a special service on the
first Sunday in Advent. Episcopal Bishop Anson Phelps
Stokes, Jr., also took part. Each of the bishops delivered

short sermons, and both Catholic and Protestant hymns and prayers were used. It was believed to have been the first such ecumenical service of its kind in this country, and was the forerunner of an Episcopal ordination service in Palmyra, Missouri, in which a Roman Catholic priest took an active part, by reading the litany.

It was characteristic that the Cardinal should observe his twentieth anniversary as archbishop, on November 9, 1964, by pursuing a routine schedule, without special notice of the occasion. He said mass for the nuns of the archepiscopal household and laid a cornerstone for a new elementary school in suburban Somerville. The school, part of a complex ranging up through high school, was operated by the Sisters of Notre Dame de Namur. And it was only natural for the prelate to get in one of his salty observations.

"Never underestimate the power of a nun," said the Cardinal at the ceremonies. "The original plans called for the elimination of the high school—until a visit from the Provincial of the Notre Dame nuns.

"Everyone knows you can never win an argument with a woman, certainly never with a mother provincial. The high school remains."

The Cardinal then exercised a prerogative of his own by ordering two extra holidays for the schoolchildren of the parish.

In spite of the recognition he had achieved and the honors that had been bestowed on him, the Cardinal continued to be outwardly unimpressed. He did not insist on his episcopal dignity nor the signs of deference due a cardinal. While he would permit the kissing of his ring under ceremonial circumstances, or by visiting priests at his residence, with other visitors he usually raised his hands over his head, or turned his ring away and shook hands firmly when he met people. He once told a group of Catholic women who came up to him at a meeting and began to kneel, "Save your knees for scrubbing the floors"—although the fashionably dressed ladies were at least two generations away from the kind of housework the Cardinal remembered from his South Boston boyhood.

The Cardinal had received an honorary degree from Harvard in 1959 and he continued to be awarded further honors. By 1964 he could count decorations from at least ten sovereign countries and two from the State of the Vatican City. In June, 1964, he went to Brandeis University with a group of other distinguished personages to receive an honorary degree from the Jewish-sponsored, nonsectarian university. The citation which accompanied his degree probably sums up his character more succinctly and cogently than a detailed account of his life. It read:

RICHARD JAMES, CARDINAL CUSHING—HONORARY DOCTOR OF HUMANE LETTERS DEGREE

FOR TWENTY YEARS ARCHBISHOP OF BOSTON, HE WEARS THE RED HAT OF THE COLLEGE OF CARDINALS IN A FASHION ALL HIS OWN. HE CHERISHES, WITH FRANCISCAN TENDERNESS, HIS SPECIAL FLOCK—THE AGED, THE UNPROTECTED, ABOVE ALL, THE EXCEPTIONAL CHILDREN. TRANSCENDING THE PAROCHIAL, HE REACHES OUT TO THE SHANTIES OF THE POOR AND THE FORGOTTEN OF LATIN AMERICA. IN AFFECTION CALLED "HIS ELEGANCE," HE WATCHED A BELOVED YOUNG FRIEND RISE TO PRESIDENTIAL EMINENCE AND SHARED WITH BURNING SORROW A FAMILY'S AND A NATION'S GRIEF. EARLY A PATRON OF THIS YOUNG UNIVERSITY, HE BLESSED AND NAMED THE BETHLEHEM CHAPEL. HIS GIFT OF MICROFILMED VATICAN HEBREW CODICES

TO THE BRANDEIS LIBRARY SYNTHESIZES HIS REVERENCE FOR THE INSEPARABLE HERITAGE OF JUDAISM AND CHRISTIANITY. WITH JOHN XXIII, HE ANNOUNCES HIMSELF TO THE JEWISH WORLD AS "JOSEPH, YOUR BROTHER," AND CARRIES FORWARD THE ECUMENICAL BANNER OF POPE PAUL. IMPATIENT AS THERESA OF AVILA, YET DESCENDED FROM PHILIP NERI, SAINT OF HOLY LAUGHTER, HE WOULD HAVE MEN DISSOLVE DISSENSION IN THE CENACLE OF THE HUMAN HEART.